HEART OF THE PALMS

FAVORITE RECIPES OF THE PALM BEACHES

PUBLISHED BY THE
JUNIOR LEAGUE
OF THE PALM BEACHES

The purpose of the Junior League of the Palm Beaches, Inc. is exclusively educational and charitable and is to promote voluntarism; to develop the potential of its members for voluntary participation in community affairs; and to demonstrate the effectiveness of trained volunteers.

Proceeds from Heart of the Palms will be used to support the league's projects within the community.

For your convenience, order forms are provided in the back of the book. Additional copies may be obtained by writing:

Junior League Publications
P.O. Box 168
Palm Beach, Florida 33480

Copyright ©1982
The Junior League of the Palm Beaches, Inc.
Palm Beach, Florida

All Rights Reserved
Library of Congress Catalog Card Number 82-80784
ISBN 0-9608090-0-7

First Printing, 1982, 10,000 copies

Cover Design and Illustrations:
Steve Allen, Gregg Dyess
The Graphic Designers Studio

Typography by American Graphics Corporation
Fort Lauderdale, Florida

Printed by Kingsport Press, Inc.
Kingsport, Tennessee

Introduction

If you have ever stood on a beach and watched coconut palms sway as the ocean lapped the shore, then you can easily relate to the magic of our area... But there is more!

Palm Beach County is vast and varied. It is blessed with fertile vegetable farms and abundant fruit trees, unending sugar cane fields and unmatched ocean smorgasboards—AND many varieties of those majestic, graceful palms.

In this semi-tropical clime entertaining is a resortful way of life, whether it is an elegant patio dinner, an impromptu picnic at the beach, hors d'oeuvres on the boat, or a simple meal on a summer day.

From the Heart of the Palms we bring you our favorite tropical flavors to capture your palate as they have ours.

Cookbook Committee

CHAIRMAN .... Debbie Price
EDITOR .... Sharon Flow
COPY EDITOR .... Phillis Jones
RECIPE CHAIRMEN .... Judi Davis
Det Gary
Jackie Jones
E.J. Murray
Becky Myers
Kim Ryan
Sandy Smith
TYPISTS .... MaryLynn Grant
Debi Middleton
Sheri Reback
ADVISORS .... Carol Milling
Shirley Moorhouse
COMMITTEE .... Patty Ahrenholz
Linda Brown
Gail Eissey
Mary Greenman
Diann Hall
Linda Jolley
Lynne Kairalla
Ann Maus
Mary Mahoney
Becky Myers
Marcia Perry
Trudy Word

Table of Contents

Hearts of Palm

Palms are undoubtedly one of Florida's greatest charms. One such tree, which is a symbol of the real Florida, is the sabal Palmetto, better known as the cabbage palm. The tender inside of this tree's thick trunk is the heart of palm. Another name for this bland, ivory-layered delicacy is swamp cabbage.

The cabbage palm is on the Florida threatened species list and may not be removed from other people's private land or public land without permission. So aside from cutting down trees on your own property, fresh sabal palm stumps can be ordered from AAA Nursery in Okeechobee, Florida, for approximately $2.50 each. This then begins an adventure in itself, as a stump must then be peeled with an ax or chain saw until the heart is exposed. Only the least fibrous center portion is desirable. The heart is white in color and it yellows quickly, so the very crumbly pieces should be put in water as soon as they are cut from the stump. One heart produces about 4 cups, serving small portions to four people.

By far the easiest way to acquire hearts of palm is to purchase them canned from your grocery store or specialty food store. Hearts of palm are produced commercially in and imported from Brazil. This canned product has been specially processed and should be treated like canned asparagus. Serve cold in a salad, mixed with your favorite dressing. The palm hearts may also be heated, drained, and served with a sauce. One 14-ounce can serves 4 or more.

Committee's Choice Chicken Salad

Salad:
½ **pound bacon, cooked, crumbled**
4 **cups white chicken meat, cooked, diced**
1 **14-ounce can hearts of palm, drained, sliced**
Lettuce leaves
4 **tomatoes, cut into 6 wedges**
24 **pitted black olives**

Combine bacon, chicken, and hearts of palm in a 2-quart bowl. Add bleu cheese dressing and mix well. Cover and refrigerate several hours. Arrange lettuce leaves on individual serving plates and top with chicken mixture. Garnish with tomato wedges and black olives. Serves 6.

Bleu Cheese Dressing:
½ **cup mayonnaise**
½ **cup sour cream**
3 **tablespoons milk**
2 **tablespoons lemon juice**
½ **teaspoon seasoned salt**
⅔ **cup bleu cheese, crumbled**

Mix mayonnaise, sour cream, milk, lemon juice, and salt in a blender for 30 seconds. Add bleu cheese and mix for a few seconds. Chill overnight. Makes 1⅓ cups.

Hearts of Palm Swamp Cabbage

2   raw hearts of sabal palm
1   onion, chopped
1   slice bacon or fat back
½   cup milk
½   cup water
¼   cup bourbon or a blended
    whisky
Salt and pepper to taste

Combine all ingredients. Simmer, adding more liquid, if necessary, for 30 to 40 minutes or until the palm is very soft. Remove bacon before serving. Serves 6.

Swamp Cabbage is a Florida tradition. Serve it with fish and hush puppies.

Hearts of Palm Antipasto

Marinade:
¼   cup wine vinegar
¼   cup vegetable oil
½   cup mayonnaise
1½ teaspoons mustard
¼   teaspoon salt
¼   teaspoon garlic powder
1½ teaspoons Worcestershire
    sauce
1   hard-cooked egg, grated
4   tablespoons chives,
    chopped

Whisk together thoroughly vinegar and oil. Add mayonnaise, mustard, salt, garlic powder, and Worcestershire sauce and continue to whisk. Fold in egg and chives.

Vegetables:
1   16-ounce can whole green
    beans
1   15-ounce can asparagus
    spears
1   14-ounce can artichoke
    hearts
1   16-ounce can small whole
    carrots
1   14-ounce can hearts of
    palm, sliced

Use the vegetables listed or any other vegetables desired. Drain vegetables and arrange separately, without mixing them, in a large 9 x 13-inch oven proof baking dish. Pour marinade over vegetables and refrigerate. To serve, arrange vegetables in wheel fashion on a large platter with hearts of palm in the center. Decorate with sprigs of parsley. Serves 16.

Hearts of Palm Salad

Salad:
2   heads bibb lettuce
3   14-ounce cans hearts of
     palm, drained
½   pound mushrooms, sliced
1   cup chopped walnuts

Arrange lettuce evenly on 4 salad plates. Arrange hearts of palm, in spoke formation, on lettuce.

Sprinkle each salad evenly with mushrooms and nuts. Spoon desired amount of dressing over salads. Serves 4.

Special French Dressing:
1   egg
1   tablespoon salt
2   tablespoons sugar
¼   teaspoon paprika
2   tablespoons brown spicy
     mustard
1   teaspoon Worcestershire
     sauce
1   garlic clove, crushed
½   cup water
1   cup wine vinegar
2   cups vegetable oil

Combine all ingredients, except oil, and mix together well. Slowly add oil, beating constantly. Chill. Makes 4 cups.

Hearts of Palm Dijon

Salad:
1 bunch watercress, washed,
     dried, chilled
1 14-ounce can hearts of palm,
     drained and sliced
2 cups sliced fresh mushrooms
1 2½-ounce package sliced
     almonds, toasted

Combine ingredients and toss with ½ cup dressing. Serves 6.

Dressing:
4   tablespoons wine vinegar
2   teaspoons Dijon-style
     mustard
1   teaspoon salt
¼   teaspoon white pepper
1   cup olive oil

Combine vinegar, mustard, salt, and pepper in a 1-quart container. Add olive oil and blend vigorously. Store in refrigerator. Bring to room temperature before serving.

Hearts of Palm au Gratin

3 cups sliced celery
1 4-ounce can sliced mushrooms, drained
1 14-ounce can hearts of palm, drained and sliced
6 tablespoons butter or margarine
4 tablespoons all-purpose flour
1 cup chicken broth
1 cup half and half
½ cup bread crumbs
½ cup grated Parmesan cheese

Cook celery in a small amount of salted water for 5 minutes. Drain. Combine celery, mushrooms, and hearts of palm and pour into a greased 2-quart casserole.

Melt 4 tablespoons butter in a saucepan and blend in flour. Gradually add broth and half and half, stirring constantly until sauce is smooth and thickened. Pour over celery mixture.

Melt remaining 2 tablespoons butter. Toss with bread crumbs and cheese. Sprinkle over top of casserole. Bake at 350 degrees for 25 minutes. Serves 6 to 8.

Herb Tomato Salad

Salad:
4 medium tomatoes, cut into wedges
1 14-ounce can hearts of palm, drained and sliced
¼ cup fresh parsley, chopped
¾ teaspoon dried basil
1 teaspoon chopped chives

Combine tomatoes and hearts of palm. Add parsley, basil, and chives. Toss lightly with ½ cup dressing. Marinate in refrigerator at least 2 hours. Serves 4 to 6.

Dressing:
6 tablespoons olive oil
2 tablespoons tarragon vinegar
1 tablespoon lemon juice
¼ teaspoon dry mustard
½ teaspoon celery salt
1 teaspoon sugar
½ teaspoon paprika
¼ teaspoon salt
¼ teaspoon pepper

Combine all ingredients; mix well.

Avocado and Hearts of Palm Salad

Salad:
1   **large avocado, peeled and sliced**
1   **14-ounce can hearts of palm, drained, chilled, sliced**
1   **11-ounce can mandarin oranges, drained, chilled**
1   **head romaine lettuce, torn into bite-size pieces**
15 **capers, optional**

Toss together ingredients in a large salad bowl. Mix with dressing. Serves 6 to 8.

Herbed Dressing:
½   **cup olive oil**
4   **tablespoons wine vinegar**
⅛   **teaspoon powdered thyme**
⅛   **teaspoon powdered marjoram**
¼   **teaspoon basil**
1   **tablespoon chopped green onion**
½   **teaspoon salt**
½   **teaspoon white pepper**
2   **tablespoons chopped fresh parsley**
½   **teaspoon Worcestershire sauce**

Combine all ingredients in a blender or processor. Makes ¾ cup.

Swamp Cabbage Fritters

2   **cups cooked and drained swamp cabbage**
1   **onion, diced**
1   **egg**
1   **cup self-rising flour**
½   **teaspoon salt**
¼   **teaspoon pepper**
Vegetable oil

Combine cabbage, onion, and egg. Gradually add flour, salt, and pepper, mixing well. Drop by tablespoonfuls into ¼ inch of hot oil and fry 4 to 5 minutes until golden brown. Makes 14 to 16 fritters.

Hearts of Palm
Italian Marinated Salad

1   14-ounce can hearts of
    palm, drained and sliced
1   bunch broccoli, separated
    into small florets
1   head cauliflower,
    separated into small florets
1   red onion, sliced
1   green pepper, sliced
2   tomatoes, cut into wedges
4   stalks celery, sliced
2   6-ounce cans pitted black
    olives, drained and sliced
½   teaspoon monosodium
    glutamate
½   teaspoon seasoned salt
2   cups Italian salad dressing

Combine all ingredients, except salad dressing, in a large mixing bowl. Pour dressing over. Cover and marinate, in refrigerator, 6 to 8 hours. Toss well. Serves 12 to 14.

A P P E T I Z E R S

Mushroom Bites

1	loaf sliced bread
1	egg yolk
1	8-ounce package cream cheese
1	4½-ounce jar mushroom stems and pieces, drained
½	medium onion, diced
1	teaspoon Worcestershire sauce

Cut 1½-inch rounds from bread. Combine the other ingredients and mound on bread rounds. Place on an ungreased cookie sheet and freeze. After rounds are frozen they may be placed in a plastic bag. When ready to serve, remove from freezer and place on an ungreased cookie sheet. Bake at 350 degrees for 20 minutes. Makes 4 dozen.

Shrimp Mold

1½	tablespoons unflavored gelatin
3	4½-ounce cans shrimp, drained, reserving liquid
1	10½-ounce can tomato soup
1	3-ounce package cream cheese, softened
½	cup chopped scallions
¾	cup minced celery
1	cup mayonnaise
¼	cup sour cream
½	teaspoon garlic powder

Soften gelatin in ¼ cup shrimp liquid. Heat tomato soup and stir in cream cheese. Add softened gelatin and stir until dissolved. Cool.

Mix remaining ingredients, except shrimp, in a blender and add to soup mixture. Mash shrimp and add to mixture. Pour into a greased 1-quart fish mold and refrigerate overnight. Serves 15 to 20.

Hungarian Sausage Meatballs

1	pound mild-seasoned sausage
3	slices bread, soaked in water and squeezed dry
¼	cup finely chopped onion
1	egg
1	small garlic clove, minced
Salt and pepper to taste	
½	cup applesauce
2	tablespoons horseradish
¼	cup sour cream

Thoroughly combine the first 6 ingredients. Shape into marble-size balls.

Combine applesauce, horseradish and sour cream. Broil sausage balls in oven for 5 to 6 minutes. Serve on toothpicks with applesauce mixture. Makes 34.

Cheese Puffs

2 3-ounce packages cream cheese
1 cup butter or margarine
1 teaspoon dry mustard
½ pound extra sharp cheese, grated
4 egg whites, stiffly beaten
1 loaf day-old unsliced white bread

Melt first 4 ingredients in top of a double boiler. Cool slightly. Fold in egg whites.

Remove crust from bread and cut bread into 1-inch cubes. Dip cubes in cheese mixture, to coat, and place cubes on a lightly greased cookie sheet. Bake at 400 degrees for about 12 minutes. Makes 4 dozen.

Cocktail Puffs

1 cup water
½ cup butter
¼ teaspoon salt
1 cup sifted all-purpose flour
4 eggs

Combine water, butter and salt in a saucepan. Bring to boil. Add flour, all at once, and stir vigorously until dough forms a ball and leaves sides of pan.

Remove from heat and cool, by beating 2 more minutes. Add eggs, one at a time, and beat vigorously after each. Continue beating until mixture is smooth. Drop by ½ teaspoonfuls onto an ungreased cookie sheet. Bake at 375 degrees for 30 minutes. Cut a slit in top of each and bake 5 more minutes.

Fill with tuna or chicken salad. Makes 65 to 70 puffs.

Layered Mexican Dip

1   large ripe avocado, peeled,
    seed removed, mashed
1   cup sour cream
¼   teaspoon chili powder
¼   teaspoon garlic powder
2   16-ounce cans refried
    beans with green chilies
1   4-ounce can chopped
    green chilies, drained
1   4-ounce can chopped black
    olives, drained
2   ripe tomatoes, peeled,
    chopped
3 or 4 green onions, chopped
1½ cups grated Cheddar
    cheese

Combine avocado, sour cream, chili powder, and garlic powder. Spread refried beans in bottom of a 2-quart deep dish. Carefully spread avocado mixture over beans. Sprinkle chilies and black olives over avocado mixture.

Layer with tomatoes, onions, and cheese, in that order. Cover and refrigerate until serving. Serve with tortilla chips. Serves 25 to 30.

Chut-Nut Crab

1   6-ounce can crabmeat
3   ounces bleu cheese,
    crumbled
½   cup chutney
1   8-ounce package cream
    cheese, softened
2   tablespoons minced onion

Microwave
Combine all ingredients in a 1½-quart casserole. Cover and microwave on high for 3 minutes, stirring once. Serve hot with crackers. Make 2 cups.

Artichoke Bites

1   cup mayonnaise
1   cup grated Parmesan
    cheese
1   14-ounce can artichoke
    hearts, sliced thin
1   6-ounce package Melba
    rounds

Combine mayonnaise and cheese. Place a slice of artichoke heart on a Melba round. Put a teaspoon of cheese mixture on top of each artichoke slice. Bake at 325 degrees for 20 minutes. Serve hot. Serves 10 to 12.

Shrimp Topped Cucumber and Cream Cheese Spread

1½ cups cucumber, peeled, finely chopped
1 8-ounce package cream cheese
¼ cup mayonnaise
¼ cup chopped onion
¼ teaspoon garlic salt
Green food coloring, optional
2 loaves whole wheat bread, cut in 2-inch circles
1 pound tiny shrimp, cooked, shelled, chilled

Blot excess water from cucumber on paper towels.

Combine cream cheese, mayonnaise, onion, garlic salt, and cucumber; tint a light green if desired. Spread mixture on bread circles. Place shrimp on top. Makes 48.

Asparagus Roll-Ups

20 slices white bread
3 ounces bleu cheese
1 8-ounce package cream cheese, softened
1 egg, beaten
1 15-ounce can asparagus spears, well drained
½ cup butter, melted

Remove crusts from bread and roll each slice flat with a rolling pin.

Combine cheeses and egg. Mix well. Spread mixture evenly on slices of bread. Place asparagus spears on each slice of bread. Roll up and secure each with toothpicks. Dip each roll in melted butter, place on a baking sheet, and freeze. When ready to use, partially thaw rolls and slice each into three equal pieces. Bake at 375 degrees for 15 minutes. Makes 60.

Hot Cheese Dip

1 cup grated Cheddar cheese
1 cup mayonnaise
1 cup chopped onion

Combine ingredients and pour into a 1-quart baking dish. Bake at 325 degrees for about 25 minutes or until bubbly and brown. Serve with assorted crackers. Serves 10 to 12.

Taco Dip

1 **6-ounce jar marinated artichoke hearts, drained and chopped**
1 **14-ounce can artichoke hearts, drained and chopped**
1 **4-ounce can green chili peppers, drained and chopped**
6 **tablespoons mayonnaise**
1½ **to 2 cups shredded Cheddar cheese**
Taco chips

Place artichoke hearts in the bottom of a 9-inch pie pan or a quiche pan. Spread chilies over top of artichokes. Cover chilies with the mayonnaise. Sprinkle cheese over mayonnaise. Bake at 350 degrees for 15 minutes or until bubbly. Serves 8.

Italian Sausage and Peppers

1 **pound hot Italian sausage, cut into 1-inch pieces**
1 **pound mild Italian sausage, cut into 1-inch pieces**
2 **tablespoons olive oil**
2 **6-ounce jars mushroom caps, drained**
1 **garlic clove, minced**
2 **tablespoons wine vinegar**
¼ **cup white wine**
1 **teaspoon salt**
¼ **teaspoon pepper**
1 **12-ounce jar fried, red peppers, drained**

Brown sausages in oil over medium heat. Add mushrooms and garlic, and sauté for several minutes. Drain excess oil. Add vinegar, wine, salt, and pepper. Add red peppers. Simmer 20 minutes. Transfer mixture to a heated chafing dish and serve with toothpicks. May be made ahead and reheated. Serves 12 to 14.

Caviar Pie

1   8-ounce package cream cheese
1   cup sour cream
2   hard-cooked eggs
2   teaspoons lemon juice
1   3½-ounce jar whitefish roe caviar
1   medium onion, minced

Combine cream cheese and sour cream and beat until smooth. Divide into 2 compote dishes. Separately chop egg whites and yolks and sprinkle with lemon juice.

Layer caviar, onion, and eggs over cream cheese mixture. Refrigerate. Serve with crackers. Serves 10 to 12.

Party Sandwiches

1   4½-ounce can chopped, black olives
6   green onions and tops, chopped
1   cup grated mild Cheddar cheese
1   cup grated sharp Cheddar cheese
½   cup mayonnaise
2   loaves party rye or pumpernickel bread

Mix all ingredients together and spread on individual slices of party breads. Bake at 350 degrees until cheese melts. Makes about 3 dozen.

Shrimp Butter

2   5-ounce cans shrimp, drained
1   tablespoon minced onion
1   tablespoon lemon juice
Dash cayenne
½   teaspoon beau monde
4   heaping tablespoons mayonnaise
¾   cup butter, softened
1   8-ounce package cream cheese
1   teaspoon dill weed

Combine all ingredients with mixer or in a blender. Serve with crackers or toast rounds. Serves 15 or more.

Shrimp Toast

**16 to 18 thin slices white
    bread, cut in half, crusts
    removed**
3 cups vegetable oil

Spread about 2½ teaspoons of shrimp paste evenly to edge of each piece of bread.

Heat oil in a large skillet or wok over medium high heat. Drop bread in, shrimp side down until edges are brown, about ½ to 1 minute. Turn bread and brown other side. Drain. Makes 32 to 36 pieces.

Shrimp Paste:
**½   pound small shrimp,
    cooked, peeled and
    deveined, finely chopped**
**3   strips bacon, finely
    chopped**
**5   water chestnuts, finely
    chopped**
**1   tablespoon chopped green
    onion**
1   tablespoon sherry
1½ teaspoon salt
½   teaspoon sugar
¼   teaspoon pepper
¼   teaspoon Accent
4   medium eggs, beaten
2   tablespoons cornstarch

Mix shrimp, bacon, water chestnuts, and green onion in a bowl. Add sherry, salt, sugar, pepper, and Accent and mix well. Add eggs and cornstarch.

Swiss Fondue

1	garlic clove
2	cups dry white wine
½	pound Swiss cheese, diced
½	pound Gruyere cheese, diced
3	tablespoons all-purpose flour
1	tablespoon lemon juice
3	tablespoons kirsch

Dash nutmeg
Dash paprika
French bread, cut in 1-inch cubes
Sliced green apples

Rub garlic around saucepan. Add wine and heat to almost a boil. Sprinkle diced cheeses with flour and mix so cubes are coated. Add cheese, a little at a time, to the wine and stir until smooth. Add lemon juice, kirsch, nutmeg, and paprika. Serve with bread and apples. Serves 4 to 6.

Mexican Queso Dip

1	pound mild Cheddar cheese, grated
1	4-ounce can green chili peppers, drained and chopped
1	egg
2	tablespoons milk

Place cheese in a 9-inch pie pan. Place chilies on top. Mix egg and milk in a bowl and pour over chilies. Bake at 425 degrees for 40 minutes. Serve with taco chips. Serves 6 to 8.

Shrimply Delicious

1	.07-ounce package Italian salad dressing mix
1	3-ounce package cream cheese
1	cup sour cream
1	teaspoon lemon juice
2	tablespoons finely chopped green pepper
1	cup cooked shrimp, shelled and deveined

Combine all ingredients. Chill 1 hour and serve with crackers. Serves 8.

Shrimp Remoulade

3   cups shrimp, boiled,
    shelled, deveined
1   cup olive oil
½   cup tarragon vinegar
1¼ cups chopped celery
¼   cup paprika
2   tablespoons horseradish
2   tablespoons chopped green
    pepper
5   tablespoons chopped
    parsley
¾   cup creole mustard
2½ teaspoons salt
½   teaspoon lemon pepper

Combine all ingredients and marinate in refrigerator for at least 24 hours. Stir often. Serves about 12.

Salmon Party Roll

1   15½-ounce can salmon,
    drained and flaked
1   8-ounce package cream
    cheese, softened
1   tablespoon lemon juice
2   teaspoons horseradish
¼   teaspoon salt
1   teaspoon liquid smoke
½   cup chopped pecans
3   tablespoons fresh, snipped
    parsley

Combine first 6 ingredients and chill. Form into a ball or log. Roll in pecans and parsley. Serve with crackers. Serves 12.

Guacamole Dip

2   **medium avocados, peeled, seeds removed**
2   **tablespoons lemon juice**
1¼ **teaspoons salt**
1   **medium tomato, peeled and diced**
½   **small onion, finely chopped**
1   **small garlic clove, minced**
1   **4-ounce can mild green chilies, drained and chopped**
Fresh coriander leaves for garnish

Mash avocado with lemon juice. Stir in salt, tomato, onion, garlic, and chilies. Spoon into a bowl and garnish with fresh coriander leaves. Serve with raw vegetables or chips. Makes about 2 cups.

Stuffed Mushrooms

1   **pound whole, fresh mushrooms**
2   **to 3 large onions, chopped**
1   **garlic clove, minced**
Parsley, salt, pepper, oregano to taste
¼   **to ½ cup grated Parmesan cheese**
2   **tablespoons butter**
1   **cup bread crumbs**
2   **tablespoons vegetable oil**

Cut stems from mushroom caps and reserve. Place caps, open side up, in a casserole. Set aide.

Chop mushroom stems. Cook stems, onion, garlic, seasonings, and cheese in a skillet with butter until lightly browned. Remove from heat and add bread crumbs.

Lightly pile mixture into mushroom caps and brush with oil. Bake at 400 degrees for 15 to 20 minutes or until mushrooms are tender and tops are browned. Serves 20.

Caviar Cheese Loaf

6   3-ounce packages cream cheese
4   tablespoons light cream
3   tablespoons horseradish
1   tablespoon salted, dried parsley
1   teaspoon whole cloves
1   medium onion, minced
2   teaspoons Worcestershire sauce
¼   teaspoon dry mustard
¼   teaspoon red pepper
1   teaspoon garlic salt
1   2-ounce jar black caviar
5   hard-cooked eggs, finely chopped

Combine all ingredients thoroughly, except the eggs and caviar. Place half of the mixture on an oval serving platter, shaping it to form the bottom half of a loaf. Refrigerate until firm. Cover the loaf with the caviar.

Finish to a rounded meat loaf shape with the other half of the mixture. Cover the exterior with an icing of very finely chopped-hard-cooked eggs and refrigerate until serving time. Serves 36.

Hot Olive Cheese Puffs

1   cup grated sharp cheese
3   tablespoons butter, softened
½   cup all-purpose flour
½   teaspoon salt
½   teaspoon paprika
Stuffed green olives

Thoroughly blend cheese, butter, flour, salt, and paprika. Mold around individual olives into small balls. Bake on an ungreased cookie sheet at 400 degrees for 15 minutes.

Refrigerate or freeze puffs until ready to bake. Serves 6.

Bleu Cheese Dip

1   heaping tablespoon beef stock base
4   ounces bleu cheese
1   medium onion, finely chopped
1   8-ounce package cream cheese
1   tablespoon Worcestershire sauce
2   cups mayonnaise

Combine the first 5 ingredients, first mashing with a fork, then blending until smooth. Fold in mayonnaise.

Serve with raw vegetables cut into bite-size pieces. Serves 8 to 10.

Gennie's Hot Crab Dip

1   8-ounce package cream
    cheese, softened
3   tablespoons mayonnaise
3   tablespoons sauterne
1   teaspoon horseradish
¼   teaspoon salt
Dash pepper
¾   cup crabmeat
2   tablespoons minced onion
1   2-ounce package slivered
    almonds, toasted

Mix well the first 6 ingredients. Add crab-meat and minced onion. Add ⅔ of the almonds to the crab dip.

Pour mixture into an oven-proof dish. Bake at 375 degrees for 15 minutes. Transfer to a warmed chafing dish and sprinkle remaining almonds on top. Serves 12.

Chafing Dish Meatballs

1   pound ground chuck
½   cup fine bread crumbs
 ⅓ cup minced onion
¼   cup milk
1   egg
1   teaspoon salt
⅛   teaspoon pepper
½   teaspoon Worcestershire
    sauce
¼   cup vegetable oil
1   12-ounce bottle chili sauce
1   10-ounce jar grape jelly

Mix first 8 ingredients and shape into 1-inch meatballs. Heat oil in skillet and brown meatballs. Remove and drain.

Heat chili sauce and jelly in a saucepan until jelly is melted. Add meatballs and stir until coated. Simmer 30 minutes. Pour into a chafing dish. Serves 20.

Crabmeat Mold

1   tablespoon unflavored gelatin
¼   cup cold water
¼   cup hot water
1   cup mayonnaise
1   cup chopped celery
1   cup crabmeat, chopped or flaked
Pinch of salt, pepper, paprika
2   green onions, finely chopped
Parsley for garnish

Dissolve gelatin in the cold water in a medium-size bowl. Stir in hot water and allow mixture to cool. Add the remaining ingredients and mix well. Pour mixture into a 4-cup mold and chill until set. Unmold onto a serving plate. Garnish with fresh parsley. Serves 8.

Marinated Antipasto

1   cauliflower head, separated into florets
2   3-ounce cans mushroom caps, drained
1   14-ounce can artichoke hearts, drained
1   7½-ounce can tiny carrots
2   teaspoons chopped pimento
⅔ cup olive oil
⅔ cup white vinegar
1   teaspoon Italian seasoning
¼   cup minced onion
1   teaspoon salt
1   teaspoon sugar
¼   teaspoon minced garlic
⅛   teaspoon ground pepper

Combine vegetables in a bowl and sprinkle pimento over mixture.

Combine remaining ingredients in a saucepan and bring to a boil. Cool slightly and pour over vegetables. Cover and refrigerate for at least 12 hours. Serves 6.

Boursin Cheese

2 8-ounce packages cream
   cheese, softened
½ cup butter or margarine,
   softened
¼ teaspoon salt
¼ teaspoon thyme
¼ teaspoon marjoram
¼ teaspoon dill
¼ teaspoon black pepper
¼ teaspoon basil

Combine cream cheese and butter. Mix in spices. Serve with crackers. Serves 10 to 12.

Artichoke Pâté

1 14-ounce can artichoke
   hearts, drained
1 8-ounce bottle Italian
   dressing
1 2-ounce jar black caviar
Mayonnaise
1 hard-cooked egg, yolk and
   white chopped fine
   separately

Marinate artichoke hearts in the Italian dressing for several hours or overnight in the refrigerator. Remove from dressing and finely chop. Divide amount into four parts. With 1 part, make a round layer in the center of serving plate about 3 or 4-inches in diameter. Spread a thin layer of mayonnaise over layer.

Spread caviar thinly and carefully over the mayonnaise. Spread on the next artichoke layer and continue, ending with an artichoke layer on top. Spread a thin layer of mayonnaise on the top and sides of the pâté cake.

Sprinkle the top with the chopped egg yolk, and press the chopped whites of egg onto the sides with the back of a spoon. Cover, without touching, with plastic wrap, Refrigerate until ready to serve. Serves 6.

"Crocked" Cheese Spread

1   **8-ounce package cream cheese, softened**
1   **5-ounce jar sharp cheese spread**
1   **tablespoon chopped green onion**
   ⅓ cup beer, at room temperature
1   **teaspoon horseradish**
1   **teaspoon Dijon-style mustard**
Green or red peppers

Microwave

Combine cheeses in a 1½-quart casserole. Microwave on high for 2½ minutes. Gradually stir in remaining ingredients. Cover and microwave on high 2 minutes, stirring twice. Refrigerate overnight. Pack cheese in a hollowed out green or red pepper, and serve with crackers. Serves 8.

Chipped Beef Dip

1   **8-ounce package cream cheese**
½   **cup sour cream**
½   **small onion, chopped**
¼   **green pepper, chopped**
1   **4-ounce package dried beef, torn into small pieces**
¼   **cup chopped pecans**

Mix all ingredients together except for pecans. Pour into a 1-quart casserole. Bake at 350 degrees for 15 minutes. Top with pecans. Serve warm with crackers. Serves 10 to 12.

Melt Away Mushrooms

1   **8-ounce package cream cheese, softened**
1   **teaspoon horseradish**
½   **pound bacon, cooked crisp and crumbled**
1   **pound fresh mushrooms, stems removed**

Combine cream cheese, horseradish, and bacon. Fill mushroom caps with cheese mixture. Place on a greased cookie sheet and bake at 325 degrees for 30 minutes. Serves 6.

Hot Clam Dip

½ cup finely chopped green
    pepper
3   tablespoons butter
1   8-ounce can clams, drained
    and minced
¼   pound hickory-smoked
    cheese
4   tablespoons catchup
1   tablespoon Worcestershire
    sauce
1   tablespoon sherry
¼   teaspoon paprika

Sauté the green pepper in butter for 3 minutes. Add the remaining ingredients. Transfer to top of a double boiler and cook until the cheese melts. Serve warm in a chafing dish with pumpernickel bread or Melba toast. Serves 8 to 10.

Pâté au Cognac

1   pound chicken livers
1   medium onion, chopped
2   tablespoons butter
¼   cup chicken broth, heated
1   tablespoon Worcestershire
    sauce
½   teaspoon paprika
¼   to ½ teaspoon curry
    powder
⅛   teaspoon pepper
2   tablespoons cognac
½   cup unsalted butter,
    softened

Sauté chicken livers with onions in 2 tablespoons butter until lightly brown. Add broth and simmer gently for 5 minutes. Transfer to blender with seasonings and cognac. Blend at high speed for 15 seconds. Add softened butter, a little at a time, and continue blending until mixture is smooth.

Pour pâté into a bowl and chill until firm. Serve with Melba toast. Freezes well. Serves 8.

Cheese Biscuits

1   **cup butter**
½   **pound sharp Cheddar**
    cheese, grated
2   **cups all-purpose flour**
1   **egg, slightly beaten**
Pecan halves
Salt to taste

Mix butter and cheese well. Add flour. Roll out on a floured surface, cut with a round biscuit cutter, and place on a greased cookie sheet. Brush with egg and top each with a pecan half.

Bake at 350 degrees for 10 to 12 minutes. Remove from pan immediately, and generously sprinkle with salt.

Biscuits can be stored for a few weeks in an air-tight container. Serves 12 to 14.

Oyster Hors d'Oeuvres

2   **8-ounce packages cream**
    cheese
2   **cups sour cream**
1   **teaspoon Worcestershire**
    sauce
2   **3¾-ounce cans smoked**
    oysters
1   **teaspoon Dijon-style**
    mustard
1   **tablespoon lemon juice**
Dash Tabasco
Dash salt

Mix all ingredients and heat in top of a double boiler. Pour into a chafing dish and serve with crackers. Serves 18 to 20.

Hot Artichoke Dip

1   **14-ounce can artichoke**
    hearts, drained and
    chopped
1   **cup mayonnaise**
1   **cup grated Parmesan or**
    Romano cheese
½   **teaspoon garlic powder**
1   **teaspoon lemon juice**
½   **teaspoon Tabasco**

Combine all ingredients, mixing well. Bake in a greased 1-quart baking dish at 350 degrees for 20 minutes. Serves 8 to 12.

Hot Chicken Dip

1 10¾-ounce can cream of
   mushroom soup
1 6½-ounce can boned
   chicken, chopped
1 8-ounce package cream
   cheese
1 4-ounce can mushrooms,
   drained, chopped
½ 2¾-ounce package
   blanched almonds
  ⅓ cup Worcestershire sauce
Garlic powder to taste

Combine all ingredients. Serve hot with
corn chips. Serves 15 to 20.

Crabmeat Surprise

1 10¾-ounce can cream of
   chicken soup
  ⅓ cup milk or white wine
1 egg, slightly beaten
1½ cups frozen crabmeat, well
   drained
¾ pound grated sharp
   Cheddar cheese
¼ cup minced onion
⅛ teaspoon Worcestershire
   sauce

Simmer soup with milk or wine. Stir in egg.
Add remaining ingredients and mix well.
Bring to a boil. Serve hot with toast rounds.
Serves 20 to 25.

Dried Beef Florentine

1	10-ounce package frozen, chopped spinach
1	8-ounce package cream cheese, softened
½	cup mayonnaise
2	tablespoons milk
2	tablespoons finely chopped onion
1	garlic clove, minced
1	2½-ounce package dried beef, chopped
¾	cup chopped pecans
2	teaspoons dried dill
1	cup sour cream

Microwave

Microwave spinach on high in a covered 1½-quart casserole for 6 to 7 minutes, stirring after first 3 minutes. Drain well.

Place cream cheese, mayonnaise, milk, onion, and garlic in a 1½-quart covered casserole and microwave on high for 2 minutes. Add beef and pecans to cheese mixture, along with dill and sour cream. Cover and microwave on high for 4 minutes, stirring after first 2 minutes. Serve hot with assorted crackers. Makes 3¼ cups.

Dill Dip

1	cup sour cream
½	cup mayonnaise
1	teaspoon grated onion
1	tablespoon dried parsley flakes
1	teaspoon dried dill weed
1	teaspoon beau monde seasoning

Mix together all ingredients. Chill. Serve with raw vegetables, crackers or potato chips. Makes about 1½ cups.

Breakfast Nut Rolls

1¼ cups milk
1 package active dry yeast
2 cups butter, softened
6 cups all-purpose flour
6 tablespoons sugar
Pinch of salt
6 egg yolks
¼ cup water
Confectioners' sugar
1 egg white, beaten
Sugar

Scald milk. Cool to lukewarm. Add yeast, stirring to dissolve. Combine butter, flour, 6 tablespoons sugar, salt, egg yolks, and water in a large bowl. Blend in the yeast mixture with a fork, working dough until it holds together.

Divide dough into 6 small balls; wrap in waxed paper and chill overnight in the refrigerator.

Roll out each ball of dough into a rectangle, ¼-inch thick, on a board covered with confectioners' sugar. Baste each rectangle with 1/6 of the filling. Roll each rectangle lengthwise, jelly roll fashion. Brush dough with the beaten egg white and sprinkle with sugar.

Place rolls on cookie sheets, seam-side down. Bake at 350 degrees for 35 minutes. Makes 6 rolls of 10 slices each.

Filling:
6 egg whites
2⅔ cups light brown sugar
4 cups ground walnuts or
   pecans

Beat egg whites until foamy. Add brown sugar and nuts.

Island Banana Bread

1¼ cups all-purpose flour
1 cup sugar
½ teaspoon salt
1 teaspoon baking soda
½ cup butter
3 ripe bananas, mashed
2 eggs, well beaten

Sift together dry ingredients. Work butter in, by hand, until mixture is crumbly. Add the mashed bananas and quickly add eggs, being careful not to overmix. Mixture should be lumpy.

Pour batter into a greased 9 x 5-inch loaf pan. Bake at 350 degrees for 45 minutes. Makes 1 loaf.

Marble Coffee Cake

Cake:

1½ cups sugar
1   cup butter
4   eggs, separated
3   cups all-purpose flour
½   teaspoon salt
3   teaspoons baking powder
1   cup milk
3   tablespoons butter

Cream 1 cup sugar with 1 cup butter, until light, in a large bowl. Add egg yolks and beat. Sift together flour, salt, and baking powder and add alternately with milk to batter. Beat egg whites until stiff. Add ½ cup sugar. Fold mixture into batter.

Alternate layers of batter and cocoa filling into a greased 10-inch tube pan. Cut through with a knife to mix. Dot top with 3 tablespoons butter. Bake at 375 degrees for 1 hour. Makes 1 cake.

Filling:

½   cup sugar
1   tablespoon cocoa
1   teaspoon cinnamon

Combine all ingredients in a small bowl.

Shoofly Cake

4   cups all-purpose flour
2   cups sugar
1   cup vegetable oil
1   teaspoon salt
½   cup dark molasses
½   cup dark corn syrup
2   cups boiling water
2   teaspoons baking soda

Mix flour, sugar, oil, and salt into a coarse crumb mixture in a bowl. Reserve 1 cup of mixture.

Combine remaining ingredients with reserved crumb mixture and pour into a 9 x 13-inch pan. Top with reserved crumb mixture. Bake at 350 degrees for 35 to 40 minutes. Serve warm. Makes 1 cake.

Cinnamon Popovers

3   eggs
1   cup milk
1   cup all-purpose flour
3   tablespoons butter, melted
1   teaspoon cinnamon
2   tablespoons sugar
¼   teaspoon salt
Hot butter or apple jelly

Combine the first 7 ingredients in a blender. Cover and blend for 30 seconds. Spoon into a well greased muffin tin, filling ½ full. Bake at 400 degrees for 40 minutes. Remove popovers from tin and fill with hot butter or apple jelly. Makes 8 to 12.

Cherry Nut Bread

2   cups all-purpose flour
1½ teaspoons baking powder
1   teaspoon baking soda
½   teaspoon salt
4   tablespoons butter, softened
1   cup brown sugar
1   egg
¾   cup buttermilk
¼   cup maraschino cherry juice
½   cup chopped nuts
½   cup chopped maraschino cherries

Sift flour, baking powder, soda, and salt together. Cream the butter and sugar. Add the egg and mix well. Add dry ingredients and liquids to the creamed mixture. Stir in nuts and cherries. Pour into a greased 9 x 5-inch loaf pan. Bake at 325 degrees for 50 to 60 minutes. Makes 1 loaf.

Pita Bread Beau Monde

6 to 8 small pita bread rounds
6 tablespoons butter, softened
Beau monde seasoning to taste

Split pita bread rounds. Cut each circle crosswise into fourths. Spread each wedge with butter and then sprinkle with beau monde seasoning. Place bread pieces on the rack of a preheated oven. Bake at 350 degrees for 5 to 10 minutes or until brown. Makes 24 to 32 wedges.

Banana Fritters

1 cup sifted all-purpose flour
2 teaspoons baking powder
1¼ teaspoons salt
¼ cup sugar
1 egg, well beaten
⅓ cup milk
2 teaspoons butter, melted
2 to 3 bananas
¼ cup all-purpose flour, for
    coating
Vegetable oil for frying

Sift together the flour, baking powder, salt and sugar. Combine the egg and milk. Add butter. Combine egg mixture with dry ingredients and mix well.

Peel bananas and cut each into 3 to 4 diagonal slices. Roll each piece in flour, shaking off excess. Dip banana into the batter, completely coating each. Fry in hot oil 4 to 6 minutes, turning fritter to brown evenly. Drain on paper towels. Serves 6.

Gingerbread

½ cup sugar
3 cups all-purpose flour
2 teaspoons baking soda
½ teaspoon ginger
½ teaspoon salt
½ cup butter
1 cup molasses
1 cup buttermilk
2 eggs

Sift together dry ingredients. Combine butter, molasses, buttermilk, and eggs, beating until light and smooth. Pour into a greased 10-inch bundt pan. Bake at 350 degrees for 25 minutes. Serve with sauce. Serves 12.

Sauce:
1 cup brown sugar
2 tablespoons butter
¼ teaspoon salt
1 teaspoon nutmeg
1 teaspoon ground cloves
1 teaspoon cinnamon
½ cup sherry or 1 teaspoon
    vanilla and 1 cup hot water
¼ cup seeded raisins
1 teaspoon grated orange
    rind

Combine sugar, butter, salt, and spices in a saucepan, stirring until mixture reaches a boil. Add sherry and boil 5 minutes. Add raisins and orange rind and cook 1 minute. Serve hot over the gingerbread.

Avocado Loaf

¾   cup butter
2   cups sugar
3   eggs
2   cups all-purpose flour
⅓   cup cocoa
¾   teaspoon allspice
¾   teaspoon cinnamon
¾   teaspoon salt
1½ teaspoons baking soda
1½ cups mashed ripe avocado
¾   cup buttermilk
½   cup chopped dates
½   cup raisins
½   cup chopped walnuts

Cream butter. Slowly add sugar, beating until light and fluffy. Add eggs, one at a time, beating well.

Sift dry ingredients together, reserving ¼ cup. Fold dry ingredients into egg mixture, alternating with the mashed avocado and buttermilk.

Combine reserved ¼ cup dry ingredients with the dates, raisins and nuts; add to egg mixture. Pour batter into 2 greased 8¼ x 4½-inch loaf pans. Bake at 350 degrees for 1 hour and 5 minutes. Makes 2 loaves.

Topping, optional:
Corn syrup
Pecan halves

Brush top of loaves with corn syrup and press pecans on top. Broil until topping bubbles.

Hush Puppies

2   cups yellow cornmeal
1   tablespoon all-purpose
    flour
2   teaspoons baking powder
½   teaspoon salt
1   egg, beaten
¾   cup water
1   small onion, finely
    chopped
Vegetable oil, heated

Sift together cornmeal, flour, baking powder and salt. Combine egg, water, and onion in a bowl. Add egg mixture to dry ingredients.

Using a spoon that has first been dipped in hot oil, drop batter into deep, 350-degree oil for 1 minute. Fry 6 hush puppies at a time; lift out with a slotted spoon and drain. Makes 20.

Spoon Bread

2   cups milk
⅔   cup white cornmeal
4   tablespoons butter
1   teaspoon salt
3   eggs, separated

Heat milk in the top of a double boiler until milk forms a skim on top. Do not stir. Add cornmeal, butter, and salt, and stir until mixture thickens. Remove pan from heat.

Beat egg yolks with a fork and add to batter, stirring quickly.

Beat egg whites until stiff and gently fold into the batter. Pour batter into a greased 1½-quart casserole. Bake at 350 degrees for 45 minutes. Serves 8.

Orange Muffins

½   cup sugar
¼   cup water
½   cup grated orange rind
4   tablespoons vegetable oil
1   cup orange juice
1   egg, well beaten
2   cups sifted all-purpose
     flour
2   teaspoons baking powder
½   teaspoon salt
¼   teaspoon baking soda
4   tablespoons sugar

Combine ½ cup sugar, water, and rind in a 2-quart saucepan. Cook slowly for 5 minutes, stirring. Remove from heat. Add oil, orange juice, and egg.

Sift together remaining ingredients. Add orange mixture, stirring just enough to moisten. Batter should be lumpy. Fill greased muffin tin ⅔ full, handling as little as possible. Bake at 425 degrees for 20 to 25 minutes. Makes 20.

Old-Fashioned Nut Bread

2   cups all-purpose flour
2   teaspoons baking powder
1   teaspoon salt
1   cup sugar
1   cup milk
1   cup chopped pecans
1   egg, beaten

Sift together flour, baking powder, and salt. Add all other ingredients, except egg, and beat well. Thoroughly stir in the egg. Place dough in a greased 9 x 5-inch loaf pan and allow to rise 20 minutes. Bake at 350 degrees for 1 hour. Makes 1 loaf.

Zucchini Bread

2   cups sifted all-purpose flour
2   teaspoons baking soda
1   teaspoon salt
¼   teaspoon baking powder
3   teaspoons ground cinnamon
3   eggs
1   cup vegetable oil
1½ cups sugar
2   cups grated zucchini
2   teaspoons vanilla
1   cup chopped walnuts
1   cup raisins, optional

Sift together flour, baking soda, salt, baking powder, and cinnamon.

Combine eggs, oil, sugar, zucchini, and vanilla in a large bowl. Beat until well mixed. Stir in flour mixture. Stir in nuts and the raisins, if desired. Pour batter into 2 greased 8½ x 4½-inch loaf pans. Bake at 350 degrees for 1 hour. Cool on a rack. Makes 2 loaves.

Quick Orange Bread

3   cups Bisquick
¾   cup sugar
2   eggs
1¼ cups orange juice
1   tablespoon grated orange rind

Combine all ingredients in a large bowl and beat thoroughly for 30 seconds. Pour into 2 greased 9 x 4½-inch loaf pans. Bake at 350 degrees for 45 minutes. Makes 2 loaves.

Mango Bread

2   cups all-purpose flour
2   teaspoons baking soda
2   teaspoons cinnamon
½   teaspoon salt
3   eggs, well beaten
1½ cups sugar
½   cup chopped nuts
½   cup raisins, optional
¾   cup vegetable oil
2   cups peeled, diced mangoes

Sift together dry ingredients in a large bowl. Make a well in the center of mixture and pour in remaining ingredients. Stir until well mixed. Pour into a greased 9 x 5-inch loaf pan. Bake at 350 degrees for 1 hour, 15 minutes. Makes 1 loaf.

Garlic Toasted Beer Bread

3   cups self-rising flour or 3
     cups Bisquick
2   tablespoons sugar
1   12-ounce can beer

Combine all ingredients and knead slightly. Put into a greased 9 x 5-inch pan. Bake at 350 degrees for 1 hour.

Slice bread and spread with garlic butter. Broil slices until toasted. Makes 1 loaf bread.

Garlic Butter:
1   cup butter
1   teaspoon garlic powder

Combine ingredients in a bowl.

Pumpkin Bread

1   16-ounce can pumpkin
⅔   cup water
4   eggs
1   cup vegetable oil
3   cups sugar
1   teaspoon nutmeg
1½ teaspoons cinnamon
1½ teaspoons salt
2   teaspoons baking soda
3⅓ cups all-purpose flour

Cream together pumpkin, water, eggs, oil, and sugar. Combine dry ingredients and stir into pumpkin mixture. Pour into 3 greased 8½ x 4½-inch loaf pans, filling ½ full. Bake at 350 degrees for 1 hour. Makes 3 loaves.

Swedish Rye Bread

2½ cups orange juice
½   cup butter
¼   cup dark molasses
½   cup brown sugar
1   teaspoon anise
1   teaspoon fennel seed
Grated rind of 1 orange
1   teaspoon salt
2   packages active dry yeast
4   cups rye flour
2   cups all-purpose flour

Combine first 8 ingredients in a saucepan and bring to a boil. Cool until mixture is slightly warm to the touch. Add yeast. Add flours, beating 75 to 100 strokes. Add more flour if dough is sticky. Knead.

Cover and let rise until dough doubles in size, about 2 hours. Punch down and put dough into 3 greased 9 x 5-inch loaf pans. Let rise until dough again doubles in size, 1½ to 2 hours. Bake at 350 degrees for 50 minutes. Makes 3 loaves.

Orange Date Bread

Rind from 1 orange
1   10-ounce package dates
Boiling water
Juice from 1 orange
1   teaspoon soda
1   cup sugar
2   tablespoons vegetable oil
1   egg, beaten
1   teaspoon vanilla
2   cups all-purpose flour,
    sifted
1   teaspoon baking powder
1   teaspoon salt
½   cup chopped nuts

Grind together orange rind and the dates. Add boiling water to orange juice to measure 1 cup liquid. Pour mixture over the orange rind and dates. Add soda, sugar, oil, egg, and vanilla.

Sift the flour with the baking powder and salt. Gradually stir into the orange and date mixture. Add the nuts. Pour into a greased and floured 9 x 5-inch loaf pan. Bake at 350 degrees for 1 hour and 10 minutes. Makes 1 loaf.

Plain Yeast Rolls

1   package active dry yeast
¼   cup lukewarm water
1   egg, beaten
⅓   cup melted vegetable
    shortening
1   cup milk
¼   cup sugar
1   teaspoon salt
2½ to 2¾ cups all-purpose
    flour

Dissolve yeast in water. Combine the egg and shortening; add to the yeast mixture.

Scald the milk and mix with the sugar and salt. Cool. Stir milk into the yeast mixture. Add flour and knead until stiff. Place dough into a greased 7 x 11-inch pan and let rise, about 2 hours. Shape dough into rolls and place back in the pan, letting rolls touch. Bake at 375 degrees for 20 minutes. Serves 10 to 12.

Cheese Sticks

2   cups grated Cheddar
    cheese
½   cup butter, softened
1½ cups all-purpose flour
1   teaspoon baking powder
½   teaspoon salt
¼   teaspoon cayenne

Blend all ingredients together to form a smooth dough. Roll out onto a floured surface until dough is ¼-inch thick. Cut dough into 5-inch long strips. Twist each strip to give a spiral effect.

Place on an ungreased cookie sheet. Bake at 400 degrees for 8 to 10 minutes. Makes 65 cheese sticks.

Hot Cross Buns

1¼ cups quick-cooking oats, uncooked
2¾ to 3¼ cups all-purpose flour
1 teaspoon cinnamon
2 packages active dry yeast
¼ cup warm water
1 cup warm milk
⅓ cup sugar
¼ cup vegetable oil
2 teaspoons salt
3 large eggs
1 cup raisins

Blend oats in a blender until flourlike in texture, about 1 minute. Mix with 1 cup of the flour and the cinnamon. Reserve.

Dissolve yeast in water. Gently beat together the milk, sugar, oil, salt, yeast mixture, 2 eggs, and the oat-flour mixture in a large bowl. Beat for 3 minutes at medium speed, scraping the bowl. Stir in raisins and enough of the remaining flour to make a moderately stiff batter. Cover bowl and let dough rise in a warm place until almost doubled in size, about 1½ hours. Stir. Batter will be very sticky.

Turn batter onto a generously floured surface. With a covered rolling pin, roll dough to ½-inch thick. Cut dough with a 2½-inch round cutter. With floured hands, shape each round into a smooth ball and place well apart on a greased cookie sheet. Cover and let rise until again almost doubled, about 1 hour.

Beat the remaining egg just until foamy and brush each bun, making sure egg does not drip onto pan. Bake at 375 degrees for 12 to 15 minutes or until golden brown. Remove to a wire rack and cool completely.

From the tip of a small metal spatula, drop frosting to form a cross over the top of each bun. Makes 2 dozen.

Frosting:
½ cup confectioners' sugar
2 tablespoons unsalted butter, softened
¼ teaspoon vanilla
½ teaspoon milk

Combine ingredients and mix to a smooth consistency in a small bowl.

Blueberry Muffins

1   **cup sugar**
¼   **cup butter, softened**
2   **eggs, separated**
1   **cup milk**
2   **cups all-purpose flour**
1   **tablespoon baking powder**
1   **cup fresh blueberries**

Cream sugar and butter. Add egg yolks and mix. Slowly stir in milk. Add flour, reserving ¼ cup. Gently mix in the baking powder by hand. Do not overmix or muffins will be roughly textured. Batter should be lumpy.

Dredge blueberries in reserved ¼ cup flour and fold into muffin mixture.

Beat egg whites until stiff and fold into batter. Pour batter into greased and lightly floured muffin tin, filling ⅔ full. Bake at 350 degrees for 20 to 25 minutes. Makes 1½ dozen.

Healthy Bran Muffins

2   **cups all-purpose flour**
2   **cups whole wheat flour**
1   **cup soy flour**
2   **teaspoons salt**
3   **cups sugar**
5   **teaspoons baking soda**
1   **cup wheat germ**
1   **cup bran cereal**
1   **cup vegetable oil**
2   **cups apple juice**
4   **eggs, slightly beaten**
1   **quart buttermilk**
2   **cups raisins**

Combine the first 6 ingredients in a large bowl.

Combine wheat germ, cereal, oil and apple juice in a saucepan. Bring mixture to a boil and add to dry ingredients.

Combine eggs, buttermilk, and raisins in a separate bowl. Mix into apple juice-flour mixture, stirring well. Fill muffin tin ⅔ full. Bake at 400 degrees for 15 to 20 minutes. Batter will keep, covered, in the refrigerator up to 6 weeks. Makes 8 dozen.

Homemade White Bread

3¾ cups very warm water
3   packages active dry yeast
⅓   cup honey
4 to 5 teaspoons salt
8   tablespoons butter, melted
2   eggs, room temperature
10   cups all-purpose flour

Combine the water and yeast in a large 12-inch plastic bowl with a cover. Add honey, salt, butter, and eggs, beating with a mixer. Add flour, 1 cup at a time. The last 2 or 3 cups of flour will need to be mixed in with a large wooden spoon.

Place a greased lid on bowl and let dough stand in a warm place for 2 hours. Separate dough into 4 equal parts. Shape each part into a loaf and place into 4 greased 9 x 5-inch loaf pans. Cover pans and keep out of drafts for 40 minutes or until dough has doubled in size. Bake at 350 degrees for 40 minutes. Makes 4 loaves.

Cranberry Nut Loaf

2   cups all-purpose flour
1½ teaspoons baking powder
1   teaspoon salt
½   teaspoon baking soda
1   egg
¼   cup butter, softened
¾   cup orange juice
Grated rind of ½ orange
1   cup sugar
1   cup cranberries
1   cup chopped nuts

Sift first 4 ingredients together and set aside. Blend egg, butter, orange juice, rind, and sugar in a blender. Add cranberries and nuts to the blender and mix until berries and nuts are chopped fine. Pour into flour mixture and mix by hand, only until flour is moistened. Pour into a greased 9 x 5-inch loaf pan. Bake at 350 degrees for 50 to 60 minutes. Makes 1 loaf.

Papaya Bread

1   cup sugar
½   cup butter
2   eggs
1   cup mashed ripe papaya
¼   cup chopped nuts
½   cup raisins
1½ cups all-purpose flour
¼   teaspoon baking powder
1   teaspoon baking soda
½   teaspoon salt
½   teaspoon allspice
½   teaspoon cinnamon
½   teaspoon ginger

Cream sugar and butter until light. Add eggs and beat until fluffy. Add papaya, nuts, and raisins and mix all ingredients.

Sift together remaining ingredients and add to the butter mixture. Pour batter into a waxed paper lined 9 x 5-inch loaf pan. Bake at 325 degrees for 1 hour and 5 minutes. Makes 1 loaf.

Breakfast Funnel Cakes

1½ cups all-purpose flour
2   tablespoons sugar
1   teaspoon baking soda
¾   teaspoon baking powder
1   egg
¾   cup milk
2   cups vegetable oil
Confectioners' sugar

Combine dry ingredients, except confectioners' sugar. Combine egg and milk and mix into dry ingredients.

Heat enough oil to 400 degrees in a large, heavy skillet to cover bottom, 1-inch deep.

Holding a finger over the bottom of a funnel, fill funnel with ½ cup batter. Remove finger and release batter into hot oil in a spiral motion, beginning in the center and working outwards. Fry 2 to 3 minutes on one side. Turn cake and cook 1 more minute. Drain cakes on paper towels and sprinkle with confectioners' sugar. Makes 8.

Cake Doughnuts

1 cup sugar
2 eggs, beaten
3½ cups all-purpose flour
4 teaspoons baking powder
1 teaspoon salt
½ teaspoon nutmeg
2 tablespoons butter, melted
1 3-pound can vegetable
   shortening
½ cup confectioners' sugar

Gradually add 1 cup sugar to eggs and beat until mixture is thick.

Sift together flour, baking powder, salt, and nutmeg in a separate bowl. Add the egg mixture and then the melted butter and stir well. Cover and set aside 15 minutes or overnight.

Roll out ½ of the dough to ½-inch thickness. Cut dough with a well-floured doughnut cutter.

Heat shortening in a deep fat fryer to 365 degrees. Fry doughnuts for 2 minutes or until they reach desired darkness. Remove doughnuts and cool slightly. Sprinkle confectioners' sugar over warm doughnuts. Repeat procedure for second half of dough. Makes 3 to 4 dozen.

Dill Bread

1 package active dry yeast
¼ cup warm water
1 cup creamed cottage
   cheese, lukewarm
2 tablespoons sugar
1 tablespoon butter, melted
1 tablespoon finely chopped
   onion
2 teaspoons dill seed
1 teaspoon salt
¼ teaspoon baking soda
1 egg, slightly beaten
2¼ to 2½ cups all-purpose
   flour
3 tablespoons butter, melted
Salt

Dissolve yeast in warm water. Combine cottage cheese, sugar, butter, onion, dill seed, salt, and baking soda in a large bowl. Add yeast. Add egg. Gradually beat in flour until batter is stiff. Cover bowl and let dough rise until it is doubled in size, about 2 hours. Knead dough and put into a well-buttered 1½ to 2-quart casserole or a 9 x 5-inch loaf pan. Cover and let dough rise again for 45 minutes to 1 hour. Bake at 350 degrees for 40 to 50 minutes.

Bread should be golden brown and sound hollow when thumped. Brush with melted butter and sprinkle with salt. Makes 1 loaf.

Cream Cheese Bubble

2 3-ounce packages cream cheese
2 7.5-ounce cans biscuits
½ cup sugar
1 teaspoon cinnamon
3 tablespoons butter, melted
⅓ cup chopped pecans

Divide and cut cream cheese into 20 pieces and roll each piece into a ball. Separate biscuits and form into 3-inch diameter circles.

Combine sugar and cinnamon. Place 1 teaspoon cinnamon mixture and 1 cheese ball in center of each biscuit, pull together sides and pinch to seal.

Pour butter, nuts, and ½ of remaining cinnamon mixture into a 10-inch bundt or tube pan. Place ½ of the rolls on top of mixture, seam side up. Repeat layers. Bake at 375 degrees for 20 minutes. Cool 5 minutes. Invert onto a serving plate. Serves 14 to 16.

Baking Powder Biscuits

2 cups all-purpose flour
4 teaspoons baking powder
½ teaspoon salt
¼ cup butter
¾ cup milk
All-purpose flour

Sift together 2 cups flour, baking powder, and salt in a bowl. Cut in butter until mixture has the texture of cornmeal. Add milk and stir lightly with a fork until dough holds together well.

Place dough on a lightly floured board, sprinkle lightly with flour, and gently fold a few times until the surface is no longer sticky.

Roll dough to ¾-inch thickness. Using a 1 to 1½-inch biscuit cutter, cut dough into rounds. Arrange biscuits on an ungreased 9 x 11-inch baking sheet. Place on the center rack of the oven and bake at 450 degrees for 12 to 15 minutes. Makes 25 biscuits.

Vichyssoise

3	large potatoes, peeled
4	leeks
2	cups milk
1	cup water
Salt and pepper to taste	
Dash curry powder	
1	13-ounce can chicken broth
2	cups cream
Worcestershire sauce to taste	
Pinch of paprika	
Accent to taste	
Chives for garnish	

Cook potatoes and leeks in combined milk and water, over low heat, until vegetables are soft. Add salt and pepper to taste. Cool.

Puree mixture in blender with curry powder. Add chicken broth, cream, and seasonings. Chill. Serve cold in thoroughly chilled cups. Garnish with chives. Serves 8.

Old Fashion Vegetable Soup

2	to 3 pounds short ribs of beef
3	stalks celery, cut in chunks
3	large carrots, chopped
2	medium onions, chopped
1	1 pound, 13-ounce can tomatoes
½	teaspoon basil
½	teaspoon thyme
½	teaspoon marjoram
½	cup chopped, fresh parsley
1½	tablespoons salt
½	teaspoon pepper
½	pound fresh lima beans or 1 10-ounce package frozen lima beans
½	pound fresh green peas or 1 10-ounce package frozen green peas
3	ears fresh corn, kernels removed

Cover ribs with water in a large pot. Bring to a boil. Add celery, carrots, and onions. Stir in tomatoes and spices. Cover and cook over low heat 2 to 3 hours. Skim off extra fat.

Thirty minutes before serving add limas, peas, and corn. Serves 6 to 8.

Cream of Corn Soup

2   tablespoons butter
1   medium onion, chopped
8   celery stalks, chopped
2   17-ounce cans cream-style
    corn
4   cups milk
Salt and pepper to taste
Dash Tabasco

Melt butter in a 2½-quart saucepan. Add onion and celery and cook over medium heat until onion is soft. Add corn and milk. Simmer over low heat for 30 minutes. Season with salt, pepper and Tabasco. Serves 6 to 8.

Blender Broccoli Soup

1   bunch fresh broccoli,
    trimmed
3   cups chicken stock
2   egg yolks, beaten
1   cup light cream
Salt and pepper to taste
Thin lemon slices for garnish

Simmer broccoli in stock 7 to 10 minutes or until just tender. Cool slightly. Pour into blender and puree until smooth. Add egg yolks and blend; add cream. Season with salt and pepper. Chill. Garnish with thin lemon slices. Serves 6.

Sherried Crab Soup

2   cups cooked crabmeat
1   cup sherry
2   10¾-ounce cans split pea
    soup
2   10¾-ounce cans tomato
    soup
2   cups light cream
4   tablespoons fresh, chopped
    parsley
Dash curry powder
Salt and pepper to taste

Marinate crabmeat in shery for 1 hour.
Combine soups and cream in top of a double boiler. Heat just to simmering, stirring occasionally. Add crabmeat mixture, sherry, parsley, and seasonings. Serve hot. Serves 8.

Cream of Mussell Soup

2 pounds fresh mussels
1 cup dry white wine
5 to 6 sprigs parsley
2 bay leaves
1 garlic clove, minced
2 cups milk
6 egg yolks, beaten
1 cup heavy cream
1 tablespoon butter
1 teaspoon salt

Combine mussels in skillet with wine, parsley, bay leaves, and garlic. Cover and cook over high heat until mussels begin to open. Strain stock and reserve.

Remove mussels from shells and trim beard. Transfer stock to saucepan. Add mussels and milk. Bring just to boiling point. Add egg yolks, cream, butter, and salt. Heat just to a boil. Serves 4.

Black Bean Soup

2 cups dried black beans
2 quarts cold water
2 cups diced, cooked ham
4 garlic cloves, crushed
2 onions, finely chopped
2 green peppers, finely chopped
2 teaspoons salt
2 bay leaves
¼ teaspoon thyme
⅛ teaspoon cayenne
¼ teaspoon oregano
¼ teaspoon curry powder
3 tablespoons wine vinegar
½ cup white wine, rum, or sherry
Sour cream for garnish

Soak beans in water overnight or boil beans 2 minutes and let soak, covered, for 1 hour. Drain. Rinse beans thoroughly. Add remaining ingredients, except wine and sour cream, to beans in a soup kettle. Cover and simmer 2½ hours.

Cool enough to pour into a blender; puree. Stir in wine, rum, or sherry. Reheat soup. Garnish with sour cream. Serves 4.

Cold Melon Soup

1 large cantaloupe
⅓ teaspoon ground cinnamon
2¼ cups orange juice
2 tablespoons lime juice

Remove seeds from melon and cut pulp into cubes. Place melon cubes, cinnamon, and ¼ cup orange juice in a blender. Puree.

Combine remaining orange juice and lime juice and stir into puree. Chill. Serves 6.

Guadalajara Soup

2   medium cucumbers,
    peeled, halved lengthwise,
    seeded
2   avocados, peeled, seeds
    removed
2   cups frozen corn, cooked
5   medium, very juicy
    tomatoes, peeled, seeded,
    and finely chopped
1   teaspoon salt
½   teaspoon freshly ground
    pepper
Canned or homemade hot chili
    salsa
Tomato juice

Cut cucumber and avocado into small pieces and combine with corn in a large bowl. Add tomatoes, salt, and pepper and mix well. Add chili salsa to taste. If tomatoes are not juicy, add some tomato juice. Refrigerate 1 hour. Serves 10 to 12.

Salsa:
2   ripe tomatoes, seeded and
    chopped
¾   cup finely chopped onion
Chopped fresh coriander
    leaves or chopped fresh
    parsley
1 to 4 tablespoons chopped,
    fresh green chili peppers
Salt to taste

Combine all ingredients in a bowl.

Oyster Stew

2   tablespoons all-purpose
    flour
1½ teaspoons salt
⅛   teaspoon pepper
2   tablespoons water
1   pint oysters with liquid
1   quart milk, scalded
4   tablespoons butter

Combine flour, salt, pepper, and water in a saucepan and blend to a smooth paste. Stir in oysters and their liquid. Simmer over very low heat until edges of oysters curl.

Pour oyster mixture into hot milk. Remove from heat. Cover and let stand 15 minutes. Add butter. Reheat stew to serving temperature. Serves 4.

Chilled Orange Carrot Soup

2   tablespoons butter
½   teaspoon fresh minced
     ginger
1   pound thinly sliced carrots
½   cup sliced leeks, white part
     only
3   cups chicken broth
1½ cups fresh orange juice
Salt and pepper
Orange slices, grated carrot,
     and fresh mint for garnish

Melt butter in a large saucepan. Add ginger, carrots and leeks and sauté until leeks are soft but not brown. Add 2 cups chicken broth. Cover and simmer until carrots are tender, about 30 minutes.

Pour carrot mixture into a blender and blend for a few seconds. Return mixture to saucepan. Stir in remaining 1 cup chicken broth and enough orange juice to produce desired consistency. Season to taste with salt and pepper. Chill. Garnish each serving with orange slices, grated carrot, and mint. Serves 6.

Our Town Clam Chowder

2   cups peeled, cubed, white
     potatoes
2   cups diced onion
2   cups diced celery
1   cup butter or margarine
1   cup all-purpose flour
6   cups milk
2   8-ounce bottles clam juice
2   6½-ounce cans chopped
     clams, undrained
2   cups diced green pepper
2   teaspoons salt
½   teaspoon white pepper
½   teaspoon powdered thyme

Steam potatoes for 12 minutes. Sauté onion and celery in butter in a large Dutch oven for 10 minutes or until tender. Stir in flour until smooth.

Combine milk and clam juice in a saucepan and bring to a boil. Add to flour mixture, stirring constantly until smooth, about 10 minutes. Add remaining ingredients. Gently fold in potatoes. Simmer over low heat for 30 minutes. Serves 8.

Cold Cream of Celery Soup

¼   cup coarsely chopped
     onion
⅓   cup butter
2   cups diced celery
1   cup peeled, diced potatoes
1   cup chicken stock
1   bay leaf
Salt and pepper to taste
2   cups milk
½   cup heavy cream
6   tablespoons fresh parsley

Sauté onion in butter in a saucepan until soft. Add celery, potatoes, chicken stock, bay leaf, salt, and pepper. Cover and cook slowly 30 minutes or until vegetables are tender. Remove bay leaf.

Pour mixture into a blender. Add 2 cups milk and blend until smooth. Adjust seasonings. Stir in cream. Chill. Garnish with parsley. Serves 4.

Summer Soup

1   cup sour cream
1   cup light cream
2   10½-ounce cans cream of
     chicken soup
1   10-ounce package frozen
     chopped spinach, cooked,
     drained
2   celery stalks, cut into
     fourths
1   cucumber, partially peeled,
     seeds removed
1   carrot, cut into fourths
1   garlic clove
½   cup fresh parsley
½   teaspoon seasoned salt
⅛   teaspoon white pepper
Thin cucumber slices for
     garnish

Combine all ingredients, except cucumber slices, in food processor or blender. If using blender, divide in half and do each batch separately.

Process until vegetables are pureed. Cover and refrigerate overnight. Serve very cold. Garnish with thin slices of cucumber. Serves 6 to 8.

Cold Tomato Soup

6   red tomatoes, peeled,
    quartered, seeded
1   small onion, chopped
½ tablespoon fresh basil or ¼
    teaspoon dried basil
1   tablespoon sugar
Salt and pepper to taste
½ cup dry vermouth, sherry,
    or white wine
Sour cream for garnish
Chives for garnish

Heat tomatoes, onion, basil, sugar, salt, and pepper in top of a covered double boiler for 15 minutes. Pour into a blender and blend. Add choice of vermouth, sherry, or white wine. Chill thoroughly. Serve topped with sour cream, sprinkled with chives. Serves 4.

Cheese Soup

1   cup grated carrots
1   cup minced celery
½ cup minced onion
1½ quarts chicken stock or 5
    10-ounce cans chicken
    stock
2   cups milk
1   cup butter
1   cup all-purpose flour
¾ pound sharp Cheddar
    cheese, shredded
1   teaspoon salt
½ teaspoon white pepper
2   tablespoons
    Worcestershire sauce

Combine carrots, celery, onion, and chicken stock in a 4-quart pot and boil until vegetables are tender. Add milk; set aside.

Melt butter in a 2½-quart saucepan. Add flour and cook over low heat 2 to 3 minutes, stirring constantly. Add 3 to 4 cups of stock mixture, beating with a wire whisk while cooking until smooth. Slowly pour mixture back into the original pot of stock. Bring soup to a boil.

Add cheese, salt, pepper, and Worcestershire sauce. Stir only until cheese is melted. Serve hot. Serves 6 to 8.

Chilled Crab Bisque

⅓ cup finely chopped celery
¼ cup butter or margarine
3 tablespoons all-purpose flour
1 teaspoon salt
4 cups milk
1 7½-ounce can crabmeat, drained and flaked
1 tablespoon lemon juice
1 teaspoon curry powder
1 cup heavy cream

Microwave

Sauté celery in butter in a 2-quart casserole on high for 3 minutes until celery is tender. Blend in flour and salt. Add milk gradually, using a wire whisk, until blended. Microwave on high 4 minutes, stirring twice, until smooth and thick. Cool.

Add remaining ingredients to celery mixture. Stir gently to blend. Chill 6 hours. Serves 6.

Cold Cucumber Soup

3 tablespoons butter
3 large cucumbers, peeled, seeded, chopped
¼ cup chopped onion
3 tablespoons all-purpose flour
3 cups chicken stock
2 teaspoons lemon juice
1 cup heavy cream
Salt and pepper to taste
Thin slices unpeeled cucumber for garnish
Sour cream for garnish

Melt butter in a 2½-quart saucepan. Add chopped cucumber and onion; cook until soft. Stir in flour and cook slowly 3 minutes, stirring constantly. Add chicken stock and lemon juice, blending well. Simmer 2 to 3 minutes.

Pour into a blender and blend until smooth. Add cream, salt, and pepper to taste. Chill. Serve cold, garnished with a thin slice of cucumber and a dash of sour cream. Serves 6 to 8.

SALADS

Crab and Avocado Salad

Salad:
3   **large avocados, peeled, and cut into 1-inch cubes**
2½ **pounds cooked lump crabmeat**
½   **cup finely chopped celery**
½   **cup thinly sliced radishes**
¼   **cup lemon juice**
¼   **cup vinegar**
3   **tablespoons olive oil**
2   **tablespoons finely chopped green onion**
¼   **teaspoon cayenne**
1   **teaspoon Worcestershire sauce**
Salt to taste
Bibb or Boston lettuce leaves and hearts

Combine all ingredients, except lettuce. Mound onto a serving dish and surround with bibb or Boston lettuce. Serve with Louis Dressing. Serves 12.

Louis Dressing:
1   **cup mayonnaise**
¼   **cup chili sauce**
2   **tablespoons chopped parsley**
1   **tablespoon finely chopped onion**
1   **tablespoon chopped chives**
Dash cayenne
¼   **cup heavy cream, whipped**

Mix together ingredients. Chill. Makes 1½ cups.

Florida Ranch Salad

2 pounds cooked rare roast beef, cut into julienne strips
1 green pepper, thinly sliced
1 medium onion, thinly sliced
1 2-ounce can anchovies, drained and minced
½ teaspoon salt
⅛ teaspoon red pepper
1 teaspoon dry mustard
1 tablespoon soy sauce
1 tablespoon grated lemon rind
1 tablespoon chopped fresh mint
3 tablespoons vegetable oil
2 tablespoons lemon juice

Place beef, green pepper, and onion slices in a bowl. Blend together remaining ingredients, and toss with beef and vegetables. Chill at least 1 hour or overnight. Serve on individual plates. Can also be served as a filling in sandwich buns. Serves 8.

Pink Delight Frozen Salad

1 3-ounce package cream cheese, softened
¼ cup mayonnaise
1 8¼-ounce can crushed pineapple, drained
1 6¼-ounce package miniature marshmallows
1 6-ounce bottle maraschino cherries, drained and chopped.
¼ cup chopped pecans
1 drop red food coloring, optional
1 cup heavy cream, whipped

Combine cream cheese and mayonnaise. Add pineapple, marshmallows, cherries, and pecans to cream cheese mixture. Add food coloring, if desired. Fold in whipped cream. Pour into a 9 x 13-inch dish and freeze overnight. Serves 8 to 10.

German Potato Salad

12 medium-size baking
    potatoes
Salt and pepper to taste
1   large Bermuda onion,
    thinly sliced
¾ pound bacon
1   heaping tablespoon all-
    purpose flour
¾ cup dark brown sugar
⅔ cup water
⅓ cup vinegar

Boil potatoes in skins until tender. Peel and slice. Season with salt and pepper. Alternately layer potato and onion slices in a large salad bowl.

Fry bacon until crisp and chop into small bits. Leave grease in pan. Stir in flour and brown sugar. Combine water and vinegar and add, with bacon, to flour mixture. Heat and stir. Just before serving, pour mixture over potatoes and onions and stir gently. Serves 10.

Cauliflower Coleslaw

Salad:
1   medium head cauliflower,
    thinly sliced
1   cup thinly sliced radishes
1 small onion, grated
½ cup snipped watercress
¾ teaspoon salt
Dash pepper
Additional watercress for
    garnish
Radish roses for garnish

Combine vegetables and seasonings. Toss with salad dressing. Garnish with extra watercress and radish roses. Serves 10.

Dressing:
1   cup sour cream
½ .07-ounce package dry
    cheese-garlic salad
    dressing mix
1½ tablespoons lemon juice
¼ teaspoon seasoned salt
2   tablespoons vegetable oil

Combine all ingredients and serve with salad.

Holiday Fruit Salad

1   20-ounce can pineapple
    chunks, drained
1   17-ounce jar dark, sweet
    cherries, drained, pitted
1   cup chopped pecans
2   cups miniature
    marshmallows
1   cup heavy cream, whipped
3   egg yolks
4   tablespoons sugar
Juice of ½ lemon
½   teaspoon grated lemon
    rind

Combine pineapple and cherries with pecans, marshmallows, and whipped cream.

Combine remaining ingredients in the top of a double boiler. Stir constantly, over low heat, until mixture thickens and coats a spoon. Cool and add to fruit mixture. Refrigerate at least 12 hours. Serves 12.

Cauliflower Salad

1   head cauliflower, trimmed
    and separated into florets
½   cup mayonnaise
¼   teaspoon rosemary
¼   teaspoon dill
¼   teaspoon chives
1   tablespoon lemon juice
1   teaspoon Worcestershire
    sauce
1   tomato, sliced
1   green pepper, sliced
Watercress for garnish
1   Bermuda onion, sliced and
    separated into rings for
    garnish

Microwave

Place cauliflower in a 2½-quart casserole. Microwave on high for 7 minutes, stirring after 3½ minutes. Drain well and cool.

Combine next 6 ingredients in a bowl and blend well. Pour over cauliflower. Add tomato and green pepper slices. Toss lightly. Pour into a serving bowl and garnish with watercress and onion rings. Refrigerate 4 to 5 hours. Serves 4 to 6.

Curried French Salad Dressing

½ cup red wine vinegar
1 teaspoon sugar
2 tablespoons catchup
2 teaspoons salt
½ teaspoon pepper
½ teaspoon dried tarragon
½ teaspoon curry powder
Juice of 1 lemon
1 tablespoon grated yellow
   onion
¼ teaspoon Worcestershire
   sauce
4 drops Tabasco
1 cup peanut oil

Blend all ingredients, except peanut oil, for 1 minute in a blender or food processor until salt is dissolved. Add peanut oil and again blend for 1 minute. Refrigerate. Makes 2 cups.

Perkie's Salad

1 15½-ounce can French-
   style green beans, drained
1 17-ounce can tiny peas,
   drained
1 teaspoon garlic powder
10 tablespoons mayonnaise
1 medium onion, thinly
   sliced
2 teaspoons sugar
2 teaspoons seasoned salt
½ teaspoon pepper
5 bacon slices, cooked,
   crumbled

Spread half of green beans and half of peas in a shallow 1½-quart dish. Sprinkle with garlic powder. Spread 5 tablespoons mayonnaise evenly over peas. Place half of sliced onion over mixture. Sprinkle with 1 teaspoon sugar, 1 teaspoon salt and ¼ teaspoon pepper. Repeat layers, omitting garlic.

Garnish with bacon. Cover and leave at room temperature 1 hour. Refrigerate at least 2 hours. Toss gently before serving. Serves 6.

Rainbow Salad

1 15-ounce can kidney beans, drained
2 cups peeled and diced tomatoes
1 cucumber, peeled and diced
½ cup chopped green pepper
½ cup chopped green onion
2 cups diced sharp Cheddar cheese
¼ to ½ cup mayonnaise
Salt and pepper to taste
5 slices bacon, cooked crisp and crumbled for garnish
2 hard-cooked eggs, sliced for garnish

Toss all ingredients together, except bacon and egg slices, in a large salad bowl. Top with crumbled bacon and eggs. Serves 6 to 8.

Grapefruit Salad in the Shell

2 large grapefruit
⅔ cup pineapple juice
1 6-ounce package lemon-flavored gelatin
⅓ cup evaporated milk
2 ounces cream cheese, softened
1 tablespoon mayonnaise

Microwave

Halve 2 grapefruit. Remove pulp and fruit. Add pineapple juice to fruit and microwave on high for 5 minutes or until boiling. Add gelatin and cool.

Clean out membrane from grapefruit shells and fill with fruit-gelatin mixture, leaving ½-inch brim. Reserve ¼ cup gelatin mixture. Whip evaporated milk, beat in cream cheese, mayonnaise, and ¼ cup reserved gelatin mixture. Spoon over filled shells. Refrigerate and cut each shell in half when firm. Serves 8.

Frosted Cranberry Mold

1	8-ounce jar red maraschino cherries
1	3-ounce package cherry-flavored gelatin
1	16-ounce can jellied cranberry sauce
4	tablespoons lemon juice
1	cup heavy cream
3	tablespoons sugar
¼	teaspoon grated lemon rind
½	cup mayonnaise
⅓	cup chopped nuts

Drain cherries, reserving syrup. Chop cherries and set aside. Add enough water to syrup to measure 1½ cups. Heat to boiling point then add to gelatin to dissolve. Add cranberry sauce and 3 tablespoons of the lemon juice. Beat slowly, with electric mixer, until mixture is blended. Chill until slightly thickened and fold in chopped cherries. Pour into a lightly greased 6-cup mold. Freeze until firm.

Whip cream with sugar and lemon rind until stiff. Fold in remaining tablespoon lemon juice. Add mayonnaise and nuts. Freeze until firm. Serves 10.

Broccoli Mold

1	large bunch fresh broccoli
1	envelope unflavored gelatin
1	10½-ounce can beef consomme
6	hard-cooked eggs, finely chopped
½	teaspoon salt
¾	cup mayonnaise
2	tablespoons Worcestershire sauce
8	drops Tabasco

Trim broccoli, reserving only the florets. Place broccoli in rapidly boiling, salted water for 3 minutes. Drain. Dissolve gelatin in ¼ cup of the consomme. In a small saucepan, bring the remaining consomme to a boil. Add the dissolved gelatin mixture and stir well. Refrigerate 15 or 20 minutes until slightly thickened.

Combine gelatin mixture with broccoli, eggs, salt, mayonnaise, Worcestershire sauce, and Tabasco. Pour into a lightly greased 6-cup ring mold. Chill until set. Serves 6 to 8.

Cold Salmon Salad

2 envelopes unflavored
  gelatin
¾ cup cold water
¼ cup caper juice
½ cup capers
3 cups chopped celery
1 cup mayonnaise
2 1-pound cans salmon,
  drained

Sprinkle gelatin over cold water in a small saucepan. Place over low heat and stir constantly until gelatin dissolves, about 3 minutes. Remove from heat.

Combine and mix lightly with remaining ingredients. Pour into a greased 1½-quart mold; chill until firm. Unmold onto a serving plate. Serves 12.

Egg Curry Mold

2½ envelopes unflavored
  gelatin
2½ cups cold chicken broth
1 tablespoon curry powder
1½ cups mayonnaise
3 hard-cooked eggs, finely
  chopped
Watercress

Soften gelatin in ½ cup chicken broth.

Bring to a boil the 2 remaining cups of broth. Stir in curry powder and gelatin mixture. Refrigerate until mixture begins to thicken. Add mayonnaise and eggs and blend in a blender until smooth. Pour into a greased 6-cup mold and refrigerate until firm. Unmold and garnish with watercress. Serves 6 to 8.

Sara Ruth's Eggs

12 to 15 hard-cooked eggs,
  peeled and sliced
  lengthwise
Salt and pepper to taste

Place egg slices on a large serving platter. Sprinkle with salt and pepper.

Dressing:
1 cup heavy cream
¾ cup mayonnaise
4 tablespoons Durkee's salad
  sauce
Paprika
¼ cup minced parsley

Combine ingredients. Pour over eggs and sprinkle with paprika and parsley. Chill well. Serves 12.

Blue Seas Salad Dressing

1	small onion
1	cup mayonnaise
⅓	cup vegetable oil
¼	cup catchup
2	tablespoons sugar
2	tablespoons cider vinegar
1	teaspoon mustard
½	teaspoon salt
½	teaspoon paprika
¼	teaspoon celery seed
1	cup crumbled bleu cheese

Combine all ingredients, except bleu cheese, in a blender or food processor and blend until smooth. Stir in bleu cheese. Chill. Makes 2½ cups.

Gold Coast Salad with Celery Seed Dressing

Salad:

1	avocado, peeled and sliced
1	tablespoon lemon juice
1	orange, peeled and sectioned
1	grapefruit, peeled and sectioned

Lettuce leaves

Sprinkle avocado slices with lemon juice. Arrange avocado and fruit sections on lettuce leaves on individual plates. Top with celery seed dressing. Serves 4.

Dressing:

¾	to 1 cup sugar
1	teaspoon salt
1	teaspoon dry mustard
3	tablespoons grated onion
½	teaspoon celery salt
⅓	cup white vinegar
1	cup vegetable oil
2	tablespoons celery seed

Combine first 6 ingredients in a blender on low speed. Add oil, a little at a time. Stir in celery seed. Makes 1 pint.

Salad Normande

Salad:
7   cups Boston, romaine,
    escarole, or endive lettuce
½   pound bacon, cooked crisp
    and crumbled
1   cup pecans, roasted
1   cup thinly sliced green
    apples, cored

Combine all ingredients in a large salad bowl; toss with dressing. Serves 8.

Dressing:
1   2-ounce can anchovy
    fillets, drained and mashed
1   large garlic clove, minced
Juice of 1 lemon
4   tablespoons wine vinegar
1   teaspoon salt
2   teaspoons Worcestershire
    sauce
1   teaspoon white pepper
1   teaspoon black pepper
1   sprig fresh dill, chopped
2   teaspoons capers, minced
½   cup olive oil

Combine all ingredients, except oil; mix well. Whisk in oil.

Boysenberry and Wine Salad

1   6-ounce package
    raspberry-flavored gelatin
1   cup boiling water
1   cup pineapple juice
1   17-ounce can
    boysenberries
½   cup sweet port wine
1   8¼-ounce can crushed
    pineapple
½   cup chopped walnuts

Dissolve gelatin in boiling water. Add pineapple juice. Drain 1 cup juice from boysenberries and add to the gelatin, along with wine, pineapple, drained boysenberries, and walnuts. Mix together and pour into a 6-cup mold. Chill until firm. Serves 6 to 8.

Cucumber Ring

5   medium cucumbers,
     peeled, sliced lengthwise,
     seeds removed
2¼ cups water
2   tablespoons lemon juice
4   green onions and tops,
     chopped
½   cup minced, fresh parsley
4   teaspoons Worcestershire
     sauce
1½ to 2 teaspoons salt
¼   teaspoon pepper
Dash Tabasco
1   cup mayonnaise
3   envelopes unflavored
     gelatin
1   cup heavy cream, whipped
½   cup each of fresh or
     marinated tomato wedges,
     onion rings, and cucumber
     slices

Cook cucumbers in 2 cups water, with lemon juice, until tender, about 15 minutes. Drain well. Puree in a blender with onions and parsley. Add Worcestershire sauce, salt, pepper, Tabasco, and mayonnaise and blend well.

Combine gelatin in ¼ cup water, in a pan, and heat until gelatin dissolves. Stir in cucumber mixture and chill until mixture begins to gel. Fold whipped cream into mixture. Pour into a 6-cup ring mold and chill overnight.

Unmold onto a serving plate and fill center with tomato wedges, onions and cucumbers. Serves 8.

Vegetable Salad Mold

2   3-ounce packages lemon-
     flavored gelatin
1   cup hot water
1   cup mayonnaise
1   tablespoon wine vinegar
1   teaspoon salt
1   tablespoon mustard
1   tablespoon chopped green
     pepper
1   tablespoon chopped onion
1   cup chopped celery
2   cups sliced carrots, cooked
2   cups tiny peas, cooked

Dissolve gelatin in hot water. Cool. Mix together mayonnaise, vinegar, salt, mustard, green pepper, onion, and celery. Add carrots and peas. Fold in gelatin. Pour into a 2-quart dish and refrigerate until set. Serves 12.

Apricot Salad Mold

2 3-ounce packages orange-
   flavored gelatin
2 cups boiling water
1 17-ounce can peeled
   apricots
1 6¼-ounce package
   miniature marshmallows
1 cup heavy cream, whipped

Dissolve gelatin in boiling water and then allow to cool and partly set. Beat with electric mixer. Mash apricots and add pulp and juice to mixture. Add marshmallows and beat on low speed of mixer. Slowly beat in whipped cream. Pour into a 5-cup mold and refrigerate until set. Serves 12 to 16.

Sweet Cherry Salad

2 17-ounce cans dark, sweet
   cherries, pitted
1 15¼-ounce can crushed
   pineapple
2 3-ounce packages cherry-
   flavored gelatin
1 12-ounce can cola
2 3-ounce packages cream
   cheese
1 cup pecan pieces

Drain cherries and pineapple, reserving juice. Heat the juice and pour over gelatin to dissolve. Add cola and fruits. Break cream cheese into small chunks and add to mixture. Stir in pecans. Pour into a 9 x 13-inch dish and refrigerate until congealed. Serves 12 to 15.

Tomato Aspic

2 envelopes unflavored
   gelatin
½ cup cold tomato juice
3½ cups hot tomato juice
1 teaspoon Worcestershire
   sauce
Juice of ½ lemon
1 teaspoon basil
1 cup cooked, peeled, and
   deveined, chopped shrimp
½ cup chopped celery
¼ cup chopped green pepper
¼ cup chopped green olives

Soften gelatin in cold tomato juice. Dissolve mixture in heated tomato juice. Add Worcestershire sauce, lemon juice, and basil. Refrigerate until partially set.

Add remaining ingredients. Pour into a 2-quart mold. Chill until set. Unmold onto a serving plate. Serves 8 to 10.

Melon Salad

Salad:
2   small cantaloupes or
     crenshaw melons
1   cucumber, peeled, seeded
     and cut into 1-inch long
     strips
1   cup seedless green grapes
3   medium tomatoes, peeled,
     seeded, and cut in strips
2   tablespoons chopped, fresh
     mint

Cut melons in half, discard seeds and scoop out the flesh with a ball cutter. Scrape shells clean and chill.

Combine melon balls, cucumber, grapes, and tomatoes in a bowl. Pour dressing over salad and mix gently. Taste and adjust seasoning. Cover and chill up to 6 hours.

To serve, mix mint with salad. Spoon into melon shells and place on individual plates. Serves 4.

Dressing:
2   tablespoons lemon juice
1   tablespoon sugar
Salt and pepper to taste
2   tablespoons vegetable oil
¼   cup light cream

Whisk lemon juice with sugar, salt, and pepper until sugar and salt are dissolved. Whisk in the oil, a little at a time, followed by the cream, so the dressing emulsifies and thickens slightly.

Salad of Artichoke Bottoms and Mushrooms

4   tablespoons wine vinegar
4   tablespoons olive oil
 ¾   teaspoon salt
½   teaspoon pepper
1   tablespoon chopped chives
     or parsley
2   14-ounce cans artichoke
     bottoms, drained
2   tablespoons lemon juice
1   cup heavy cream
1   tablespoon dry mustard
1   garlic clove, finely
     chopped
1   pound fresh mushrooms,
     thinly sliced
Lettuce

Pour 2 tablespoons vinegar, 2 tablespoons olive oil, ½ teaspoon salt, ¼ teaspoon pepper, and chives over artichoke bottoms. Cover and marinate several hours. Whisk lemon juice and 2 tablespoons vinegar with ¼ teaspoon salt and ¼ teaspoon pepper. Gradually whisk in the cream. Add mustard and garlic. Pour mixture over mushrooms and mix well. Cover tightly and marinate 2 or more hours.

To serve, arrange artichokes on bed of lettuce and pile mushrooms in center of artichokes. Serves 12.

Chicken Chutney Salad

2   cups diced, cooked chicken
    breasts
1   8-ounce can pineapple
    chunks, drained and sliced
1   cup diagonally sliced
    celery
½   cup sliced green onions
⅔   cup mayonnaise
2   tablespoons chopped
    chutney
½   teaspoon lemon rind
2   tablespoons lemon juice
1   teaspoon sugar
½   teaspoon curry powder
¼   teaspoon salt
½   cup sliced almonds
Lettuce leaves

Combine all ingredients, except almonds and lettuce. Mix with 2 forks, working up and down slowly.

Roast sliced almonds in a 350-degree oven for 2 minutes until golden. Serve salad on lettuce leaves and garnish with almonds. Serves 4.

Tony's Caesar Salad

2   heads romaine lettuce,
    chilled, torn into bite-size
    pieces
1   cup croutons

Pour dressing over lettuce in a large salad bowl. Toss well. Add croutons. Serves 12.

Dressing:
½   cup olive oil
1   egg
2   tablespoons lemon juice
1   teaspoon Worcestershire
    sauce
1   garlic clove
5   anchovy fillets
½   teaspoon salt
¼   teaspoon pepper
½   cup Parmesan cheese
¼   cup crumbled bleu cheese

Blend all ingredients in a blender or food processor for 6 to 10 seconds.

Dilly Lima Bean Salad

1 10-ounce package frozen
   baby lima beans
2 tablespoons chopped, fresh
   parsley
½ cup chopped celery
2 tablespoons mayonnaise
2 tablespoons sour cream
2 tablespoons vinegar
½ teaspoon dill seed
6 slices bacon, cooked,
   crumbled

Microwave
Microwave lima beans according to package directions. Drain. Add remaining ingredients and mix well. Refrigerate overnight. Serves 4.

Sea Island Salad

Salad:
1 cup cooked crabmeat
1 cup cooked shrimp, peeled,
   deveined
¼ cup chopped onion
1 cup chopped celery
½ cup water chestnuts, sliced
1 cup fresh pineapple chunks
½ cup chopped cashew nuts
6 tablespoons currants
4 tablespoons chutney
½ teaspoon salt
Juice of 1 key lime
Lettuce leaves

Combine all ingredients, except lettuce, in a bowl. Refrigerate 3 hours. Arrange lettuce leaves on individual plates and top with salad mixture. Spoon 3 to 4 tablespoons dressing over each salad. Serves 6.

Dressing:
1 cup mayonnaise
¼ cup sour cream
½ teaspoon curry powder

Combine all ingredients. Refrigerate 3 hours.

Mandarin Spinach Salad

Salad:
- ½   **pound bacon**
- 1   **2½-ounce package sliced almonds**
- 1   **10-ounce package fresh spinach, washed, stems removed, chilled**
- 1   **11-ounce can mandarin oranges, drained, chilled**

Dressing:
- 1   **cup catchup**
- 1   **cup vegetable oil**
- ⅔   **cup vinegar**
- ⅔   **cup sugar**
- 1   **small grated onion, optional**
- 1   **teaspoon salt**
- 1   **teaspoon celery seed**
- ½   **teaspoon paprika**
- **Juice of 1 lemon**
- 1   **garlic clove, minced**
- **Pinch of dry mustard**
- ½   **teaspoon Worcestershire sauce**

Microwave

Cook bacon until crisp. Drain, crumble, and set aside. Sauté almonds in bacon grease over medium heat until lightly brown. Drain.

In a large bowl, toss spinach and oranges. Stir in dressing. Add bacon and almonds. Serve immediately. Serves 4.

Combine first 10 ingredients in a quart jar and shake well. Add a pinch of dry mustard and Worcestershire sauce. Refrigerate. Keeps indefinitely. Makes 4 cups.

Pickled Black Eyed Peas

- 5   **15-ounce cans black-eyed peas, drained**
- 3   **3¼-ounce cans pitted black olives, drained and sliced**
- 1   **cup sliced red onions**
- 1   **garlic clove, minced**
- 2   **cups vegetable oil**
- ¾   **cup red wine vinegar**
- 1   **tablespoon parsley**
- ⅛   **teaspoon Tabasco**
- **Salt and pepper to taste**

Combine peas, olives, onions, and garlic. Separately mix together the remaining ingredients and pour over vegetable mixture. Refrigerate, covered, for at least 24 hours. Serves 16 to 20.

Zucchini Salad with Tarragon Garlic Dressing

Salad:
1   small head romaine
      lettuce
1   small head Boston lettuce
1   pound zucchini, peeled and
      sliced
1   cup sliced radishes
3   tablespoons sliced green
      onions

Wash, dry and chill lettuce greens. Toss with zucchini, radishes and onion. Chill. Serves 8.

Dressing:
¼   cup vegetable oil
3   tablespoons tarragon
      vinegar
2   teaspoons salt
1   garlic clove, minced
⅛   teaspoon pepper

Combine all ingredients and mix well. Pour over chilled salad vegetables.

Outdoor Potato Salad

½   pound bacon, diced
¾   cup chopped onion
⅓   cup chopped green pepper
6   cups cubed, cooked
      potatoes
⅓   cup chopped pimento
¾   cup mayonnaise
¼   cup mustard
¼   cup sugar
1   teaspoon salt
⅛   teaspoon pepper

Cook bacon, onion, and green pepper together until bacon is crisp. Drain. Add to remaining ingredients and toss lightly.

Pour mixture onto a double thickness of heavy foil and wrap securely. Place foil package on a grill, over hot coals, and cook 20 to 30 minutes, turning occasionally. Serves 6.

Chinese Slaw

Slaw:
1   3-ounce package noodles
    from chicken-flavored
    Oodles of Noodles
1   medium head cabbage,
    sliced
½   cup slivered almonds,
    toasted
3   tablespoons sesame seeds,
    toasted

Crush noodles and combine with cabbage, almonds, and sesame seeds. Pour dressing over mixture and toss well. Marinate overnight in refrigerator. Serves 6 to 8.

Dressing:
2   tablespoons sugar
4   tablespoons cider vinegar
½   cup vegetable oil
¼   teaspoon seasoned salt
¼   teaspoon Worcestershire
    sauce
¼   teaspoon pepper
**Seasoning package from
    chicken-flavored Oodles of
    Noodles**

Combine all ingredients and mix well.

Tiny Tender Pea Salad

6   tablespoons mayonnaise
Juice of 1 lemon
1   small onion, chopped
1   10-ounce package tiny
    peas
1   cup shredded Cheddar
    cheese
2   cups Boston or romaine
    lettuce
6   slices bacon, cooked crisp,
    crumbled

Combine mayonnaise, lemon juice, onion, peas, and cheese. Cover and refrigerate 24 hours.

To serve, add lettuce and crumbled bacon. Toss well in a salad bowl. Serves 6.

Mushroom Bacon Salad

1 pound fresh mushrooms, thinly sliced
3 green onions and tops, thinly sliced
⅔ cup olive or vegetable oil
4 tablespoons lemon juice
1 teaspoon Worcestershire sauce
½ teaspoon salt
⅛ teaspoon pepper
½ teaspoon dry mustard
12 slices bacon, cooked crisp, crumbled
1 head Boston or bibb lettuce

Place mushrooms in a bowl. Combine next 7 ingredients. Mix until well blended. Pour over mushrooms and stir gently. Cover and refrigerate at least 4 hours or overnight.

Line a serving bowl with lettuce leaves. Spoon mushroom mixture onto lettuce. Sprinkle bacon on top. Serves 4 to 6.

Marinated Asparagus

2 pounds fresh asparagus spears

Trim asparagus; steam for 5 minutes or until tender-crisp. Drain and arrange in a 9 x 13-inch dish.

Dressing:
½ cup wine vinegar
½ cup water
½ cup vegetable oil
1 teaspoon brown mustard
2 teaspoons Worcestershire sauce
¼ teaspoon Accent
Salt and pepper to taste
½ large dill pickle, chopped
½ medium onion, chopped
1 hard-cooked egg, chopped
⅛ cup chopped capers
2 tablespoons chopped pimento
2 tablespoons chopped fresh parsley

Mix together first 6 ingredients; add salt and pepper. Add remaining ingredients and pour over asparagus. Cover and marinate in the refrigerator overnight. Serves 4 to 6.

Tropical Fruit Medley
with Poppy Seed Dressing

Salad:
1   pint fresh strawberries,
    stems removed, hulled
1   cantaloupe, cubed
1   honeydew, cubed
1   fresh pineapple, cubed
2   cups seedless green grapes
2   cups watermelon balls
2   cups sliced bananas

Combine all fruit, except bananas. Refrigerate to blend flavors. Just before serving add bananas and arrange fruits on individual serving plates. Drizzle with poppy seed dressing. Serves 6 to 10.

Dressing:
⅓   cup honey
¼   cup white vinegar
2   teaspoons lemon juice
¾   cup vegetable oil
½   cup sugar
1   teaspoon dry mustard
1   teaspoon paprika
1   teaspoon poppyseeds
¼   teaspoon salt

Combine honey, vinegar, lemon juice, and vegetable oil in blender or food processor for 15 seconds. Add remaining ingredients and blend for 30 seconds until spices are dissolved. Refrigerate. Makes 1 pint.

Curried Chicken Salad

Salad:
2   cups cooked chicken, cut
    into bite-size pieces
1½ cups chopped celery
1½ cups cooked rice, chilled
½   cup almonds, toasted
Sliced fresh pineapple
Coconut curls, toasted

Combine chicken, celery, rice, and almonds. Toss thoroughly with dressing. Salad is best prepared several hours before serving. Serve on sliced pineapple with toasted coconut curls sprinkled on top. Serves 6 to 8.

Dressing:
½   cup sour cream
½   cup Italian-style salad
    dressing
1   teaspoon salt
1   teaspoon curry powder

Combine all ingredients and toss with salad.

Rice and Ham Salad

1⅓ cups rice, cooked
¼ cup French dressing
¾ cup mayonnaise
2 tablespoons chopped onion
½ teaspoon salt
1 teaspoon curry powder
½ teaspoon dry mustard
Dash pepper
8 ounces cooked ham
1½ cups sliced fresh cauliflower
½ 10-ounce package frozen peas, cooked and drained
½ cup chopped celery
½ cup thinly sliced radishes
1 casaba melon or cantaloupe

Toss cooked rice with French dressing and chill.

Combine mayonnaise, onion, salt, curry powder, mustard, and pepper and add to chilled rice.

Cut ham in julienne strips. Add ham, cauliflower, peas, celery, and radishes to rice mixture.

Cut melon into rings and mound salad on top. Serves 10.

Bermuda Salad Bowl

Salad:
½ small onion
1 small head cauliflower
½ cup sliced green olives
1 small head lettuce
½ cup crumbled bleu cheese

Slice onion and separate into rings. Combine with cauliflower and olives. Pour dressing over mixture and let stand 30 minutes. Add lettuce and bleu cheese. Toss. Serves 6 to 8.

Dressing:
1 garlic clove, minced
½ teaspoon salt
½ teaspoon pepper
½ teaspoon Worcestershire sauce
1 tablespoon horseradish
½ cup vegetable oil

Combine all ingredients. Let stand 30 minutes before using with salad.

Watermelon Salad with Celery-Cheese Dressing

Salad:
3   cups watermelon balls, chilled
Lettuce leaves
½   cup chopped pecans

Arrange watermelon balls on lettuce leaves. Pour dressing over top and sprinkle with chopped pecans. Serves 6.

Celery-Cheese Dressing:
4   ounces cream cheese, softened
2   tablespoons mayonnaise
⅓   cup heavy cream, whipped
1⅓ cups thinly sliced celery

Beat cream cheese with mayonnaise, until smooth and fluffy. Fold in whipped cream. Stir in celery.

Sweet and Sour Slaw

1   cup vinegar
⅔   cup vegetable oil
1   teaspoon salt
1   cup sugar
1   teaspoon celery seed
1   head cabbage, chopped
1   green pepper, chopped
1   medium onion, chopped

Combine vinegar, oil, salt, sugar, and celery seed in a saucepan. Bring mixture to a boil and pour over chopped ingredients. Cover and chill 24 hours, stirring occasionally. Drain. Serves 8.

Stuffed Shrimp

4   tablespoons butter
1   medium onion, minced
1   green pepper, minced
1   7½-ounce can crabmeat
1   tablespoon dry sherry
1   teaspoon dry mustard
½   teaspoon salt
2   tablespoons mayonnaise
1   teaspoon Worcestershire
     sauce
24 jumbo shrimp, shelled,
     leaving tails, and deveined
½   cup grated Parmesan
     cheese
Dash paprika

Melt 2 tablespoons butter in a small sauce-pan. Add onion and pepper and cook until soft. Add white sauce, crabmeat, sherry, mustard, salt, mayonnaise, and Worcestershire sauce. Heat until well blended.

Split shrimp and open flat. Stuff shrimp with crabmeat mixture. Place shrimp in a large broiler pan and dot with remaining 2 tablespoons butter. Sprinkle with Parmesan cheese and paprika. Bake at 350 degrees for 15 minutes. Serves 4 to 6.

White Sauce:
2   tablespoons butter or
     margarine
2   tablespoons all-purpose
     flour
¼   teaspoon salt
Dash white pepper
1   cup milk

Melt butter in a saucepan over low heat. Blend in flour, salt, and white pepper. Add milk, stirring constantly until mixture thickens and bubbles. Remove from heat. Makes 1 cup.

Fish Key West

2   pounds snapper or grouper
     fillets
¾   cup mayonnaise
1   onion, thinly sliced
1   tomato, thinly sliced
1   green pepper, thinly sliced
Paprika
2   tablespoons lemon juice
3   tablespoons butter

Place fillets in a greased broiler pan. Spread mayonnaise over fillets. Layer onion, tomato, and green pepper slices over fish. Sprinkle with paprika and lemon juice. Dot with butter. Broil 8 to 10 minutes or until fish flakes easily. Serves 4.

Imperial Crab Meat

5   tablespoons butter
½   tablespoon chopped
    pimento
1   tablespoon chopped green
    pepper
5   tablespoons all-purpose
    flour
½   teaspoon salt
Dash white pepper
1   cup hot milk
1   egg yolk
¼   teaspoon dry mustard
¼   teaspoon drained capers
1½ teaspoons Worcestershire
    sauce
1   cup mayonnaise
1   pound fresh crabmeat
Paprika

Melt 1 tablespoon butter in a small pan. Add pimento and green pepper and sauté until soft. Set aside.

Melt remaining 4 tablespoons butter in a medium saucepan over low heat. Blend in flour, salt, and pepper. Add milk and cook, stirring constantly, until mixture thickens and bubbles. Add egg yolk, mustard, capers, Worcestershire sauce, sautéed pimento, and green pepper. Stir until well blended and remove from heat.

Mix in ¾ cup of mayonnaise. Fold in crabmeat. Spoon into 6 individual shells or shallow baking dishes. Spread remaining mayonnaise on top of each. Bake at 375 degrees for 30 minutes or until golden. Sprinkle with paprika. Serves 6.

Cousin Archie's Fish

2   cups all-purpose flour
Dash salt
Dash lemon pepper
3   pounds snapper or grouper
    fillets
1   cup olive oil
2   tablespoons butter
½   cup chopped onion
¼   cup chopped green pepper
½   cup chopped celery
1   7-ounce package
    cornbread stuffing,
    prepared
3   tablespoons soy sauce
3   tablespoons butter

Combine flour, salt, and lemon pepper. Dredge fish in flour mixture. Heat olive oil and butter in a large skillet. Sauté fish in skillet, over medium heat, until done on both sides. Transfer fish to a large baking dish.

In oil left in skillet, sauté onion, green pepper, and celery until tender but not brown. Pour over fish.

Crumble cornbread stuffing over vegetables and fish. Sprinkle with soy sauce and dot with butter. Bake at 350 degrees for 15 minutes or until heated through. Serves 8.

Oysters, Port and Starboard

Cream Sauce:
3   **tablespoons butter**
4   **tablespoons all-purpose**
     flour
¼   **teaspoon salt**
Dash white pepper
1   **cup milk**

Melt butter in a saucepan over low heat. Blend in flour, salt, and pepper. Slowly add milk, stirring constantly until mixture thickens and bubbles. Remove from heat.

Oysters:
1   **pint oysters with liquid**
½   **cup cooked, chopped**
     mushrooms
1   **pimento, chopped**
1   **tablespoon chopped**
     parsley
1   **hard-cooked egg, chopped**
¼   **teaspoon Worcestershire**
     sauce
Salt and pepper to taste
Cracker crumbs

Cook oysters, in their liquid, until edges curl, about 5 minutes. Strain. Cool and chop oysters.

Combine cream sauce with oysters, mushrooms, pimento, parsley, egg, and seasonings. Pour into lightly greased individual baking shells or ramekins and sprinkle with cracker crumbs. Place on a cookie sheet. Bake at 450 degrees for 10 minutes. Serve as an appetizer or an entrée. Serves 4.

Seafood Casserole

1   **10¾-ounce can cream of**
     mushroom soup
2   **tablespoons sherry**
1   **14½-ounce can green**
     asparagus spears, drained
1   **10-ounce package frozen**
     peas, slightly cooked and
     drained
1   **5½ or 6-ounce can**
     crabmeat, flaked
2   **hard-cooked eggs, sliced**
½   **cup crushed potato chips**
1   **cup grated sharp Cheddar**
     cheese

Combine mushroom soup with sherry. Layer ½ of all the ingredients and soup mixture in a 2-quart casserole. Repeat layers. Bake at 350 degrees for 30 minutes.

Shrimp Harpin

2   **pounds large shrimp, cooked, shelled, and deveined**
1   **teaspoon lemon juice**
3   **teaspoons vegetable oil**
¼   **cup minced green pepper**
¼   **cup minced onion**
1   **teaspoon butter**
1   **teaspoon salt**
⅛   **teaspoon pepper**
⅛   **teaspoon mace**
Dash cayenne
1   **10¾-ounce can tomato soup**
1   **cup heavy cream**
½   **cup sherry**
¾   **cup long-grain rice, cooked**
½   **cup slivered almonds**
Paprika

Place shrimp in a 2-quart casserole. Sprinkle with lemon juice and oil. Cover and refrigerate overnight.

Sauté green pepper and onion in butter until tender, about 5 minutes. Add salt, pepper, mace, cayenne, soup, cream, and sherry. Cover and refrigerate overnight.

Combine rice, prepared sauce, and ¼ cup almonds with shrimp in casserole. Top with remaining almonds and sprinkle with paprika. Bake uncovered at 350 degrees for 35 minutes. Serves 6 to 8.

Scallops au Gratin

2   **pounds bay scallops**
½   **cup white wine**
½   **teaspoon salt**
Dash cayenne
¼   **cup minced onion**
5   **tablespoons butter, melted**
3   **tablespoons all-purpose flour**
½   **cup heavy cream**
1   **cup grated sharp Cheddar cheese**
½   **cup bread crumbs**
¼   **cup grated Parmesan cheese**

Combine scallops, wine, salt, cayenne, and onion in a saucepan and bring to a boil over medium heat. Cover and simmer 8 to 10 minutes or until onion is tender. Drain, set aside onions and scallops, and reserve 1 cup stock.

Combine 3 tablespoons butter and flour, and stir into stock. Add cream and cook until sauce is thick. Add Cheddar cheese and stir until melted. Add scallops and onion. Pour mixture into a greased 8 x 12-inch baking dish.

Combine 2 remaining tablespoons butter, bread crumbs, and Parmesan cheese. Sprinkle over scallops. Bake at 375 degrees for 15 to 20 minutes. Serves 4 to 6.

Favorite Seafood Stuffing

25 butter-flavored crackers
½ large loaf French bread,
    crust removed
1 small onion, chopped
¼ cup butter
1 2-ounce can chopped
    mushrooms, drained
⅛ teaspoon chopped garlic
¼ cup chopped, fresh parsley
½ cup green or black
    chopped olives
1½ cups grated sharp Cheddar
    cheese
½ cup butter, melted
Salt and pepper to taste

Crush crackers and French bread in blender to make crumbs.

Sauté onion in butter until tender. Add mushrooms.

Combine crumbs, onion mixture, and remaining ingredients; toss lightly. Pour into a greased 7 x 11-inch casserole. Bake at 350 degrees for 20 to 25 minutes. Serve as a side dish for any seafood or as a stuffing. Serves 6 to 8.

**Stuffing for any type whole
    white fish:**

When preparing stuffing, use ¼ cup of the melted butter in the stuffing.

Lightly stuff cavity of fish. Pour remaining ¼ cup butter over fish. Bake at 350 degrees for 12 minutes per pound. Separately bake extra stuffing.

Stuffing for lobster:

When combining stuffing ingredients, use only enough of the ½ cup melted butter necessary to make stuffing slightly moist.

Split lobster lengthwise.

Remove everything, except tail meat, and fill cavity with stuffing. Pour remaining melted butter over lobster. Seal in foil. Bake at 350 degrees for 20 minutes.

Shrimp Vol-au-Vent

2 teaspoons minced onion
⅓ cup melted butter
⅓ cup all-purpose flour
1 teaspoon salt
Dash pepper
⅛ teaspoon nutmeg
1 cup milk
1 cup light cream
1 4-ounce can mushrooms, drained, liquid reserved
1 egg yolk, slightly beaten
2 pounds shrimp, cooked, peeled, and deveined
⅓ cup dry sherry
6 baked patty shells

Cook onion in melted butter, 3 minutes, over low heat in a saucepan until tender, but not brown. Blend in flour, salt, pepper, and nutmeg. Add milk, cream, and reserved mushroom liquid. Cook over medium heat, stirring constantly, until mixture is smooth and thickened.

Add a little of the hot mixture to the beaten egg yolk and blend well. Return mixture to saucepan and mix well. Cook over low heat, stirring constantly, about 3 minutes.

Combine shrimp, mushrooms, and sherry in a separate saucepan. Heat over low heat 5 minutes. Combine with sauce, stirring to blend. Pour into patty shells. Serves 6.

Seafood Diable

½ cup butter
½ pound fresh mushrooms, sliced
12 cherry tomatoes
1 cup sliced celery
1 teaspoon parsley flakes
2 teaspoons freeze-dried chives
½ teaspoon tarragon
½ teaspoon ginger
1 teaspoon dry mustard
⅛ teaspoon garlic powder
2 teaspoons seasoned salt
¼ teaspoon coarsely ground pepper
2 pounds shrimp, shelled and deveined
8 to 10 small crab claws
3 tablespoons lemon juice
¼ cup brandy, heated
4 cups cooked yellow rice

Melt butter in a large skillet. Add mushrooms, tomatoes, and celery and sauté 3 minutes. Remove and set aside.

Combine seasonings in a small bowl. Add shrimp and crab claws to skillet and sprinkle with seasonings. Sauté seafood for 2 minutes. Add lemon juice. Stir in reserved vegetables. Cover and simmer 5 minutes. Transfer to a chafing dish. Just before serving, pour heated brandy over seafood and ignite. Serve over rice. Serves 4-6.

Baked Shrimp, Mushrooms and Artichokes

White Sauce:
9   tablespoons butter
⅔   cup all-purpose flour
1½ cups milk, warmed
1½ cups heavy cream, warmed
Salt and pepper to taste
¾   cup dry sherry
**2   tablespoons
        Worcestershire sauce**

Melt butter in a heavy 1½-quart saucepan over medium heat. Add flour and cook, stirring constantly, 1 to 2 minutes. Pour in milk and cream and beat vigorously until combined.

Cook over medium heat until mixture boils and becomes thick and smooth. Add salt and pepper. Remove from heat and continue beating until cooled. Add sherry and Worcestershire sauce, combining thoroughly.

4   tablespoons butter
**1   pound mushrooms, thinly
        sliced**
**2   14-ounce can artichoke
        hearts, drained, or 2 10-
        ounce packages frozen
        artichoke hearts, cooked
        and drained**
**3   pounds shrimp, boiled,
        shelled, and deveined**
**½   cup grated Parmesan
        cheese**
Paprika

Melt butter in a large skillet over high heat. Add mushrooms and sauté until liquid evaporates and mushrooms are lightly browned.

Arrange artichokes in bottom of a buttered 3 to 4-quart baking dish. Scatter shrimp over artichokes. Spoon mushrooms over shrimp. Pour white sauce over mushrooms. Sprinkle with cheese and paprika. Bake at 375 degrees for 20 to 30 minutes. Serves 6 to 8.

Steamed Mussels

2 to 3 pounds mussels
**1½ cups white wine or
        vermouth**
1   cup water
¼   cup minced green onion
4   sprigs parsley, minced
1   small bay leaf
1   garlic clove, minced
1   cup butter, melted

Wash mussels carefully, discarding any with open shells. De-beard mussels.

Combine wine, water, onion, parsley, bay leaf, and garlic in a large kettle. Bring to a boil. Add mussels and cover kettle. Cook, stirring once, 5 to 9 minutes, until mussel shells pop open.

Skim mussels into wide soup plates. Ladle liquid over mussels. Serve with melted butter for dipping. Serves 3 to 4.

Bahamian Conch Fritters

1½ pounds conch
1 medium onion, finely chopped
2 tablespoons finely chopped green pepper
1 medium tomato, finely chopped
3 tablespoons finely chopped, tender celery parts and leaves
½ cup evaporated milk
½ cup water
2 tablespoons butter, softened
1 teaspoon salt
1 egg, well beaten
2 teaspoons baking powder
1 cup all-purpose flour
Vegetable oil

Grind conch in a meat grinder and mix with remaining ingredients in a large bowl. Drop by generous tablespoonfuls into deep hot oil. Fry until brown. Makes 40.

Crab and Spinach Casserole

½ cup onion slices
4 tablespoons butter or margarine
2 10¾-ounce cans cream of mushroom soup
½ cup grated Parmesan cheese
½ teaspoon Dijon-style mustard
2 tablespoons sherry
2 7-ounce cans crabmeat
½ pound mushrooms, sliced
2 10-ounce packages frozen, chopped spinach, cooked and drained
1 cup sour cream
1 cup fine bread crumbs
1 teaspoon chopped chives

Sauté onion in butter, in a large saucepan, until lightly browned. Add soup, cheese, mustard, and sherry, stirring constantly until mixture boils.

Stir crabmeat, mushrooms, and spinach into boiling mixture. Remove from heat. Stir in sour cream. Pour into a 2-quart casserole. Top with bread crumbs and chives. Bake at 325 degrees for 30 to 40 minutes. Serves 6 to 8.

Cracked Conch

1½ pounds conch
½ cup milk
1 cup cracker meal
Vegetable oil
Salt and pepper to taste
Tabasco to taste

Pound conch with a wooden mallet to flatten.

Dip conch into milk and then into cracker meal to coat. Cover bottom of heavy pan with oil. Fry conch over medium heat until browned, turning once. Season to taste. Serves 4.

Skewered Scallops

1 pound scallops
Salt and pepper to taste
1 cup all-purpose flour
Bay leaves
1 cup freshly made, fine bread crumbs
½ cup butter, melted

Lightly season scallops with salt and pepper. Coat scallops with flour and shake off excess.

Place scallops on 12 water soaked, wooden skewers with bay leaves inserted between every other scallop. Coat scallops with melted butter and sprinkle with bread crumbs. Grill or broil, about 3 minutes on each side. Serve as an entrée or as an appetizer. Serves 4.

Skipper's Scampi

2 cups butter
1 cup margarine
7 garlic cloves, minced
3 shallots, chopped
6 tablespoons white wine
6 tablespoons lemon juice
1 tablespoon Tabasco
1 tablespoon dry mustard
½ cup chopped chives
2½ pounds jumbo shrimp, peeled and deveined, butterflied

Melt together butter and margarine. Add garlic, shallots, wine, lemon juice, Tabasco, mustard, and chives. Simmer over low heat 3 to 4 minutes. Makes about 5 cups sauce.

Place shrimp in a broiler pan. Pour sauce over shrimp; broil 6 to 8 minutes. Serves 6.

Shrimp and Wild Rice

½ cup chopped onion
½ cup chopped green pepper
1 tablespoon butter
1 6½-ounce package wild/
  white rice, cooked
1 pound medium shrimp,
  cooked, peeled, and
  deveined
1 10¾-ounce can cream of
  mushroom soup
1 tablespoon Worcestershire
  sauce
½ 11-ounce can Cheddar
  cheese soup
1 teaspoon lemon juice
Salt and pepper to taste

Sauté onion and green pepper in butter until tender. Combine with remaining ingredients and spoon into a 2-quart casserole. Bake at 375 degrees for 35 to 40 minutes. Serves 6.

Beer Batter

2 cups all-purpose flour
1 cup beer
1 egg

Combine ingredients and allow to stand at room temperature for 1 hour.

Dip desired seafood into batter and fry until golden brown.

Shrimp Soufflé

6 slices white bread, broken
  into pieces
1 pound cooked, peeled, and
  deveined shrimp
½ pound sharp Cheddar
  cheese, grated
¼ cup butter, melted
3 eggs
½ teaspoon dry mustard
2 cups milk
Salt and pepper to taste

Arrange bread pieces, shrimp, and cheese in several layers in a buttered 2-quart casserole. Pour butter over layers.

Beat eggs and add mustard, milk, and salt and mix well. Pour mixture over casserole ingredients. Cover and let stand overnight in refrigerator. Bake at 350 degrees for 1 hour. Serves 5 to 6.

Crab Strata

8   slices buttered bread,
    crusts removed
8   slices American cheese
1   6½-ounce can crabmeat or
    tuna
1   4-ounce can mushrooms,
    drained
1   medium onion, finely
    chopped
4   eggs, beaten
2½ cups milk
1   teaspoon mustard
1   teaspoon salt

Place 4 slices of bread in bottom of an 8 x 8-inch cake pan or casserole. Layer 4 slices cheese on top of bread. Spread crabmeat or tuna over cheese. Add mushrooms and sprinkle with onion.

Place remaining 4 slices of cheese over onion and top with remaining 4 slices of bread.

Combine remaining ingredients and pour over bread. Cover and refrigerate overnight. Bake uncovered at 350 degrees for 1 hour or until firm and slightly brown. Serves 6.

Charcoal Grilled
Red Snapper Steaks

2   pounds red snapper steaks,
    cut into serving pieces
Paprika

Place fish in well greased hinged wire grills. Baste with sauce and sprinkle with paprika.

Grill 4 inches from moderately hot coals for 8 minutes. Turn fish, baste again with sauce, and sprinkle with paprika. Cook 7 to 10 minutes longer until fish flakes easily with a fork. Serves 5.

Sauce:
½   cup butter, melted
¼   cup lemon juice
2   teaspoons salt
½   teaspoon Worcestershire
    sauce
¼   teaspoon white pepper

Combine ingredients and mix well.

Caviar Crêpes

Crêpes:
2   eggs, well beaten
½   teaspoon salt
¾   to 1 cup milk
½   cup all-purpose flour

Combine eggs and salt in a bowl. Gradually add milk. Blend in the flour, until mixture is smooth. Refrigerate batter 2 hours.

Pour a tablespoon of batter into a greased, heated, 6-inch crêpe pan. Tilt to spread mixture over the pan. Brown crêpe on both sides. Repeat to make 4 dozen.

Filling:
½   teaspoon caviar, per crêpe
1   tablespoon sour cream, per crêpe

Spoon caviar and sour cream onto one end of crêpe and roll into a cylinder. Fill as many crêpes as desired and place them in a baking dish. Heat crêpes in a 350-degree oven until warm. Unused crêpes may be frozen.

Mackerel Anisette

¼   teaspoon lemon savory or coriander
¼   teaspoon ground mace
5   black peppercorns, freshly ground
5 to 6 tablespoons vegetable oil
1½ to 2 pounds mackerel or sea bass fillets
2 to 3 heads fennel
Salt to taste

Mix together lemon savory or coriander, mace, ground peppercorns, and vegetable oil. Pour over fish fillets and marinate 2 to 3 hours, turning fish several times.

Cover grill rack of an oven broiler pan with aluminum foil. Spread fennel over foil. Place marinated fish on top of fennel. Broil fish for about 8 minutes on each side. Season with salt. Serve hot or cold with remoulade sauce. Serves 4.

Remoulade Sauce:
1   cup mayonnaise
1   teaspoon chopped gherkin
1   teaspoon chopped, fresh parsley
1   teaspoon chopped tarragon
1   tablespoon Pernod

Fold together ingredients.

Stuffed Fish Casserole

1   6-ounce package stuffing
   mix, prepared
4   white-fleshed fish fillets
1   10-ounce can shrimp soup

Spread prepared stuffing in a buttered 1½-quart baking dish. Place fillets on top of stuffing. Spread soup on top of fillets. Bake at 350 degrees for 30 minutes. Serves 4.

Red Clam Sauce

1   garlic clove, crushed
1   cup chopped onion
6   tablespoons olive oil
6   tablespoons butter
⅔   cup chopped parsley
1   10-ounce can whole baby
   clams, undrained
1   cup tomato puree
4   ounces vermicelli, cooked
   drained

Sauté garlic and onion in combined olive oil and butter. Add parsley, clams, and clam juice to onion mixture. Add tomato puree. Heat, and serve over vermicelli. Serves 2 to 3.

Crab and Shrimp Casserole

2   pounds cooked Alaskan
   king crabmeat
½   pound cooked, shelled, and
   deveined shrimp
½   cup chopped green pepper
2   cups cooked brown rice
2   10-ounce packages frozen
   peas, defrosted
1½ cups mayonnaise
Seasoned salt and pepper to
   taste

Combine all ingredients and pour into a 3-quart casserole. Cover. Bake at 350 degrees for 45 to 60 minutes. Serves 8.

Crab Crêpes

Filling:
3   tablespoons chopped onion
⅔   cup butter
⅔   cup all-purpose flour
3   cups hot milk
1   teaspoon salt
¼   teaspoon white pepper
1   teaspoon dry mustard
1½ pounds crabmeat

Sauté onion in butter. Blend in flour. Gradually add hot milk, stirring constantly until smooth. Add salt and pepper. Reserve 1 cup sauce. To remaining sauce, add mustard and crabmeat. Heat thoroughly.

Crêpes:
¾   cup sifted all-purpose flour
⅛   teaspoon salt
3   eggs, beaten
2   tablespoons butter, melted
1½ cups milk
Grated Parmesan cheese

Combine all ingredients, except cheese, in a bowl and beat until smooth. Cover and let stand at room temperature about 2 hours. Butter a 6-inch crêpe pan. Pour in 3 tablespoons batter, tilting pan to spread batter. Cook crêpes until firm and lightly brown. Flip and cook the other side. Repeat until all crêpes are made.

Spread some filling evenly over each crêpe and roll up. Arrange crêpes close together in a shallow baking dish. Cover with reserved sauce. Sprinkle with Parmesan cheese. Bake at 375 degrees for 20 minutes or until heated through. Makes 18 crêpes.

Huachenanzo a la Veracruzana

3 **pounds red snapper fillets**
1 **teaspoon salt**
2 **tablespoons lime juice**

Place fillets in a single layer, in a greased 9 x 13-inch baking dish. Prick fillets with a fork and sprinkle with salt and lime juice. Set aside to season, for several hours, in refrigerator. Drain. Pour sauce over fillets. Bake at 350 degrees for 30 minutes. Serves 6.

Sauce:
1 **medium onion, thinly sliced**
1 **garlic clove, minced**
3 **tablespoons olive oil**
2 **pounds fresh tomatoes, peeled, seeded and chopped**
2 **chili jalapeno peppers, seeded and cut into strips**
12 **pitted green olives, cut in half**
½ **teaspoon salt**
¼ **teaspoon dried oregano**
2 **tablespoons large capers**
1 **large bay leaf**

Sauté onion and garlic in hot oil until tender. Add remaining ingredients. Cook over medium-high heat 5 to 10 minutes until sauce is well seasoned and some of the liquid has evaporated.

Seafood Gratin

1   pound medium-large
    shrimp, peeled and
    deveined
1   pound bay scallops
1   cup butter, melted
2   garlic cloves, minced
⅛   teaspoon ground white
    pepper
2   drops Tabasco
¼   teaspoon Worcestershire
    sauce
1   cup chopped, fresh parsley
Juice of 1½ lemons
1   cup fresh bread crumbs
2   tablespoons butter, melted

Place shrimp and scallops in a buttered 8 x 12-inch baking dish. Combine 1 cup butter, garlic, pepper, Tabasco, Worcestershire sauce, parsley, and lemon juice in a bowl. Pour mixture over shrimp and scallops. Bake at 400 degrees for 12 to 15 minutes.

Combine bread crumbs and 2 tablespoons butter and sprinkle over shrimp and scallops. Broil 2 to 3 minutes until golden brown. Serves 4 to 6.

Deviled Crab

1   cup milk
1½   tablespoons butter
1   tablespoon all-purpose
      flour
1   tablespoon chopped, fresh
      parsley
1   teaspoon salt
½   teaspoon paprika
½   teaspoon lemon juice
¼   teaspoon cayenne
¼   teaspoon mustard
1   tablespoon Worcestershire
      sauce
4   hard-cooked eggs,
      separated
1   pound crabmeat
2   tablespoons butter
Cracker crumbs, optional

Scald milk in the top of a double boiler. Combine butter and flour and stir into the milk. Add seasonings. Mash egg yolks and add to mixture.

Chop egg whites, mix with crabmeat, and fold into sauce. Pour into crab shells or ramekins. Dot with butter. Sprinkle lightly with cracker crumbs, if desired. Bake at 350 degrees until lightly brown. Serves 8.

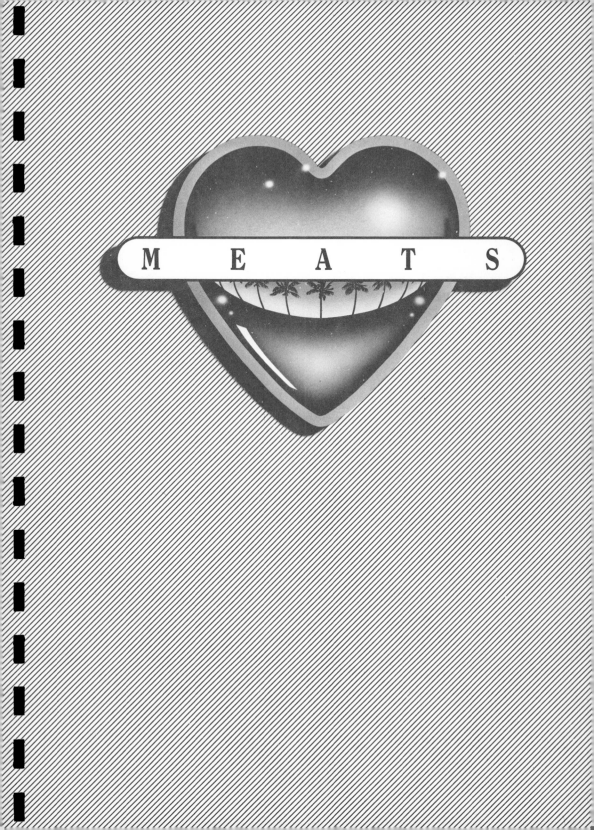

Something Extra Meatloaf

1	green pepper
1	onion
1	carrot
1	6-ounce can tomato paste
2	eggs
3	pounds ground chuck
1	cup cottage cheese
1	cup packaged dry stuffing mix
1	tablespoon Dijon mustard

Chop green pepper, onion, and carrot in a food processor. Mix in ½ of the tomato paste and the eggs. Combine vegetable mixture with the ground chuck in a large bowl, mixing well.

With hands, mix cottage cheese and stuffing into meat. Shape mixture into 1 large or 2 small meat loaves and place in a 9 x 11-inch shallow baking dish.

Combine remaining tomato paste and the mustard in a separate bowl, and spread over top of meat loaf. Bake at 350 degrees for 1½ hours. Serves 10 to 12.

Tenderloin Marsala

1	3 to 4-pound beef tenderloin
¾	cup marsala wine

Marinate tenderloin in wine for 1 hour at room temperature.

Roast or grill meat to desired doneness. Slice and serve with marsala sauce. Serves 6 to 8.

Marsala Sauce:

2	tablespoons butter
½	pound fresh mushrooms, sliced
2	tablespoons all-purpose flour
1	cup beef broth
1	teaspoon Worcestershire sauce
3	tablespoons marsala wine

Melt butter. Add mushrooms and sauté for 5 minutes. Sprinkle flour over mushrooms and add broth, Worcestershire sauce, and wine. Cook and stir until sauce is smooth and thickened. Makes 2 cups.

Moussaka

2 large eggplants, halved
   lengthwise
Salt
½ cup butter, melted
½ cup grated Parmesan
   cheese
½ cup grated Cheddar cheese
2 tablespoons dry bread
   crumbs

Slice eggplant crosswise into ½-inch pieces. Place pieces on a broiler pan, sprinkle lightly with salt, and brush with butter. Broil 4 minutes on each side or until golden brown.

Layer ½ of the eggplant, overlapping slightly, in a 2-quart baking dish. Sprinkle 2 tablespoons of the Parmesan cheese and 2 tablespoons of the Cheddar cheese over eggplant.

Stir bread crumbs into the meat sauce and spoon sauce over the eggplant. Again sprinkle with 2 tablespoons of each cheese. Layer remaining eggplant on top. Pour cream sauce over all and sprinkle with the remaining cheeses. Bake at 350 degrees for 35 to 40 minutes. Serves 6.

Meat Sauce:
2   tablespoons butter
1   cup chopped onion
1½ pounds ground chuck or
    lamb
1   garlic clove, minced
½   teaspoon oregano
1   teaspoon basil
½   teaspoon cinnamon
1   teaspoon salt
1   teaspoon pepper
2   8-ounce cans tomato sauce
1   6-ounce can tomato paste

Melt butter in a hot skillet. Sauté onion, meat, and garlic, stirring until brown, about 10 minutes. Add seasonings, tomato sauce, tomato paste, and bring to a boil, stirring. Reduce heat and simmer uncovered for 30 minutes.

Cream Sauce:
3   tablespoons butter, melted
3   tablespoons all-purpose
    flour
½   teaspoon salt
½   teaspoon pepper
2   cups milk
2   eggs, beaten

Combine butter, flour, salt, and pepper in a saucepan. Slowly add milk, stirring until thickened. Slowly beat the sauce into eggs.

Yorkshire Pudding

1   **3 to 4-pound roast beef**
2   **eggs**
1   **cup milk**
1   **cup all-purpose flour**
¼   **teaspoon salt**

Cook roast beef, removing from oven ½ hour before it is done. Cover and set aside in a warm place. Roast will continue to cook through internal heat. Reserve drippings.

Beat eggs with milk. Sift flour with salt and stir into egg mixture, beating until well blended.

Pour some of the beef drippings into a 9 x 9-inch pan or into cupcake tins. Pour batter ½-inch deep into pans. Bake at 450 degrees for 15 to 20 minutes or until puffed and brown. Serve with roast beef. Serves 8.

Steak Pinwheels

1   **1½-pound flank steak, trimmed and pounded to even thickness**
1   **teaspoon meat tenderizer**
1   **teaspoon garlic salt**
¼   **teaspoon coarsely ground black pepper**
6   **slices bacon, cooked**
2   **tablespoons chopped, fresh parsley**

Season meat with tenderizer, garlic salt, and pepper. Place bacon lengthwise on steak, and sprinkle with parsley. Roll meat lengthwise and secure with toothpicks. Slice roll into 4 even pieces. Broil or grill to desired doneness. Serves 4.

Barbecued Brisket

¼   **cup barbecue sauce**
¼   **cup chili sauce**
1   **cup tomato sauce**
1 to 2 garlic cloves, crushed
Juice of ½ lemon
½   **teaspoon Worcestershire sauce**
4   **tablespoons brown sugar**
Salt and pepper to taste
1   **4-pound beef brisket**

Combine all ingredients except brisket. Pour sauce over brisket to coat well. Cover and marinate overnight in refrigerator.

Place meat in a large roasting pan, reserving marinade, and tightly seal. Bake at 325 degrees for 4 hours. Cut meat across the grain in very thin slices. Serve with marinade sauce. Serves 6.

Company Casserole

1   pound ground beef
½   teaspoon salt
2   tablespoons butter
2   8-ounce cans tomato sauce
1   cup creamed cottage
    cheese
½   cup sour cream
⅓   cup minced onion
1   tablespoon minced green
    pepper
2   tablespoons butter, melted
1   8-ounce package cream
    cheese
1   8-ounce package wide
    noodles, cooked and
    drained

Cook ground beef with salt in 2 tablespoons butter until light brown. Add tomato sauce. Set aside.

Combine next 6 ingredients in a medium-size bowl.

Place ½ of the cooked noodles in a greased 3-quart casserole. Pour cottage cheese mixture over noodles; add the remaining noodles. Spread the meat mixture on top. Sprinkle on the topping and bake at 350 degrees for 20 minutes. Serves 8.

Topping:
1½ cups crushed corn flakes
¼   cup grated Parmesan
    cheese
2   tablespoons butter, melted
¼   teaspoon basil
¼   teaspoon onion salt
½   teaspoon oregano

Combine all ingredients.

Beef and Vegetable Fondue

2   10½-ounce cans beef broth
1   tablespoon soy sauce
Dash ground ginger
2   pounds beef tenderloin, cut
    into 1-inch cubes
½   pound fresh mushrooms
½   head cauliflower, cut into
    florets
½   head broccoli, cut into
    florets
2   zucchini, cut into chunks

Heat broth, soy sauce and ginger in a fondue pot. Spear beef cubes and assorted raw vegetables, and cook in boiling broth to desired doneness. Serve with a variety of sauces. Serves 4.

Flank Steak Marinade

Sauce:
¼ cup soy sauce
3 tablespoons honey
2 tablespoons red wine vinegar
1 teaspoon garlic powder
1½ teaspoons ginger
¾ cup vegetable oil
1 green onion, chopped

Combine sauce ingredients and pour over the steak. Cover and marinate at least 3 hours. Cook over very hot coals 5 to 10 minutes on each side. Serves 4.

1 2-pound flank steak, scored

Liver Stroganoff

1 pound calves' liver
½ cup red wine
1 cup all-purpose flour
1 bay leaf, crushed
1 teaspoon grated lemon rind
Dash thyme
4 tablespoons butter
2 tablespoons chopped onion
2 cups sour cream
½ tablespoon lemon juice
Salt and pepper to taste
2 cups sliced mushrooms
4 tablespoons chopped bacon bits
3 cups noodles, cooked and drained

Marinate liver in wine for 1 hour. Drain on paper towels. Season flour with bay leaf, lemon rind, and thyme. Coat liver lightly with flour mixture and sauté in 1 tablespoon sizzling butter. Do not overcook; meat should be rare. Place liver on a heated platter.

Sauté onion in 2 tablespoons butter. Add sour cream, lemon juice, salt, and pepper. Simmer for a few minutes.

Sauté mushrooms in 1 tablespoon butter in a separate skillet and add to the sauce. Pour sauce over liver and sprinkle with bacon bits. Serve over noodles. Serves 4 to 6.

Deluxe Short Ribs

12 2-inch short ribs
1   envelope dry onion soup
    mix
1   cup Burgundy
⅔   cup catchup
3   tablespoons soy sauce
½   teaspoon pepper
2   tablespoons brown sugar

Place ribs in a 9 x 12-inch roasting pan. Sprinkle with onion soup mix. Combine the remaining ingredients and pour over ribs. Cover and marinate in the refrigerator all day, turning ribs occasionally.

Bake at 450 degrees for 45 minutes. Reduce heat to 350 degrees and cook another 45 minutes, frequently turning ribs to soak up the sauce. Serves 4 to 6.

Beef Parmigiana

1½ pounds round steak, thinly
    sliced, and cut into serving
    pieces
1   egg, beaten
⅓   cup grated Parmesan
    cheese
⅓   cup Italian bread crumbs
⅓   cup vegetable oil
1   medium onion, chopped
¼   teaspoon pepper
1   teaspoon salt
½   teaspoon sugar
½   teaspoon oregano
½   teaspoon basil
1   6-ounce can tomato paste
2   cups hot water
½   pound Mozzarella cheese,
    sliced

Trim fat from meat and pound until about ¼-inch thick. Dip meat into egg and roll in a mixture of Parmesan cheese and bread crumbs.

Heat oil in a large skillet and brown meat on both sides. Remove meat and place in a shallow 9 x 13-inch baking dish. In the same skillet cook the onion until tender. Stir in seasonings and tomato paste. Add hot water and stir.

Pour ¾ of the sauce over meat and top with Mozzarella slices. Pour the remaining sauce over cheese. Bake at 350 degrees for 1 hour. Serves 4.

Stuffed Flank Steak

½   **pound sausage, browned
     and drained, reserving fat**
2   **cups soft bread crumbs**
1   **tablespoon minced onion**
1   **teaspoon poultry
     seasoning**
½   **cup hot water**
1   **2-pound flank steak,
     slightly pounded**
Salt and pepper to taste

Combine sausage with bread crumbs, onion, poultry seasoning, water, and 2 table-spoons reserved fat from sausage. Spread mixture on steak and roll up jelly roll fashion; tie securely in 3 or 4 places.

Place on a rack in a shallow baking pan. Bake at 350 degrees for 1 to 1½ hours. Pour pan juices over steak before servings. Serves 4 to 6.

Ground Sirloin, Etcetera

½   **pound bacon, diced**
2   **pounds ground sirloin**
1   **cup chopped onion**
1   **cup chopped celery**
1   **green pepper, chopped**
All-purpose flour
Salt and pepper to taste
1   **16-ounce can tomatoes,
     mashed**
1   **tablespoon sugar**
1   **6-ounce can tomato paste**
1   **8-ounce package noodles,
     cooked and drained**
1   **16-ounce package
     processed cheese, sliced
     thin**
1   **17-ounce can peas, drained**
1   **3-ounce can sliced
     mushrooms, drained**
1   **cup cracker crumbs**
2   **tablespoons butter**
Paprika

Fry bacon in a large skillet until crisp. Remove bacon from pan; reserve. Add ground sirloin to the bacon drippings in the pan and brown. Add onion, celery, and green pepper. Cook for about 10 minutes or until vegetables are slightly browned. Drain excess fat.

Place meat and vegetables in a greased 9 x 13-inch baking dish. All casserole ingredients are to be put together by layers, sprinkling lightly between each layer with flour, salt, and pepper.

Combine tomatoes, sugar, and tomato paste in a bowl; spread over the ground sirloin. Spread noodles over tomato mixture followed by ½ of the cheese slices. Spread the peas and then the mushrooms over cheese. Cover vegetables with the second half of the cheese. Sprinkle with bacon, followed by cracker crumbs. Dot with butter and sprinkle with paprika. Bake uncovered at 225 degrees for 1½ hours. Serves 10.

Sweet and Sour Meatballs

1½ pounds ground chuck
2 eggs
¾ cup dried bread crumbs
½ cup club soda
¼ cup minced onion
1 tablespoon salt
½ teaspoon pepper
1 tablespoon vegetable oil
2 green peppers, cut into
   1-inch pieces
2 carrots, diagonally sliced
1 15-ounce can tomato sauce
½ cup white vinegar
¼ cup sugar
1 8-ounce can pineapple
   chunks and juice
1 tablespoon cornstarch
¼ cup water
1 8-ounce can sliced water
   chestnuts, drained

Combine the first 7 ingredients in a medium size bowl and shape mixture into 1-inch meatballs. Cook meatballs until browned on all sides in oil in a large skillet. Drain meatballs.

In the same skillet, cook green peppers and carrots until tender-crisp, stirring frequently. Combine vegetables and meatballs. Add tomato sauce, vinegar, sugar, and liquid from pineapple. Heat to boiling; reduce heat to low and simmer 15 minutes.

Combine cornstarch with water in a small bowl. Gradually stir mixture into meatballs, cooking and stirring until mixture thickens and starts to boil. Add pineapple chunks and water chestnuts. Serves 8.

Escalope de Veau à la Crème

1½ pounds veal scallops
½ cup all-purpose flour
½ teaspoon salt
¼ teaspoon pepper
4 to 5 tablespoons butter
¾ cup white wine
¾ cup white veal stock
½ pound mushrooms, thinly
   sliced
½ cup heavy cream
Salt and pepper to taste
1 tablespoon chopped fresh
   parsley

Pound scallops to ¼-inch thick. Combine flour, salt, and pepper and coat scallops, patting them to remove the excess. Melt 3 tablespoons butter in a skillet and fry several of the scallops over medium heat until browned, 2 to 3 minutes on each side. Remove scallops from skillet and form an overlapping arrangement on a platter. Keep warm. Fry remaining veal in the same way, adding more butter if necessary.

Glaze pan with wine and veal stock. Add mushrooms and simmer until liquid is reduced by half and slightly thickened. Add cream and bring to a boil. Correct seasoning with salt and pepper and spoon sauce over scallops. Sprinkle with parsley. Scallops can be cooked up to 48 hours in advance and kept in the sauce in the refrigerator. Serves 4.

Veal Piccata

1 cup butter (approximately)
2 pounds veal scallops,
   pounded paper thin
All-purpose flour
¼ cup lemon juice
Salt and pepper to taste
Lemon slices for garnish
Parsley sprigs for garnish

Melt 1 teaspoon butter for each veal slice in a large, heavy skillet. Do not let butter brown. Coat veal with flour. Brown veal on both sides, over high heat, a few pieces at a time. Remove meat to a warm platter.

Add lemon juice to the skillet, season with salt and pepper, and pour over veal. Garnish with lemon slices and parsley. Serves 6.

Sautéed Veal Scallops with Lemon

1½ pounds veal scallops, cut
   3/8-inch thick
Salt
Freshly ground pepper
All-purpose flour
4 tablespoons butter
3 tablespoons olive oil
¾ cup fresh, homemade beef
   stock
6 paper-thin lemon slices
1 tablespoon lemon juice

Pound scallops to ¼-inch thick. Season with salt and pepper and dip into flour, shaking off excess. Melt 2 tablespoons butter with the oil in a heavy 12-inch skillet. When foam subsides, add veal, 4 to 5 scallops at a time, and sauté for 2 minutes on each side until golden brown. Transfer veal to a plate. Pour off fat from the skillet, leaving only a thin film on the bottom. Add ½ cup beef stock and boil briskly for 1 or 2 minutes, stirring constantly and scraping in any browned bits clinging to the bottom and sides of the pan.

Return veal to the skillet and arrange lemon slices on top. Cover and simmer over low heat for 10 to 15 minutes, or until veal is tender when pierced. Arrange veal on a heated platter and surround with the lemon slices.

Add ¼ cup of the remaining beef stock to the juices in the skillet and boil until the stock is reduced to a syrupy glaze. Add lemon juice and cook, stirring, for 1 minute. Remove pan from heat, swirl in remaining 2 tablespoons butter, and pour sauce over the scallops. Serves 4.

Veal Ruggieri

2 pounds veal scallopini
1 egg, beaten
1 cup bread crumbs
½ cup butter
½ teaspoon salt
¼ teaspoon pepper
½ teaspoon dried oregano
½ cup chicken broth
¼ to ½ cup dry sherry
1 6-ounce jar sliced
   mushrooms, drained
1 14-ounce can artichoke
   hearts, drained and halved
1 5.7-ounce can pitted black
   olives, drained and halved
1 16-ounce package
   fettuccini, cooked

Dip veal in egg and then into bread crumbs to coat. Melt butter in a large skillet and sauté veal several minutes on each side. Stir in salt, pepper, oregano, broth, and sherry. Add mushrooms, artichokes, and olives. Simmer 10 minutes. Serve with fettuccini. Serves 6.

Veal Napoli

2 pounds veal round steak,
   cut ½ to ¾-inch thick
2 teaspoons salt
1 teaspoon pepper
¾ cup all-purpose flour
3 tablespoons butter
3 tablespoons vegetable oil
1 pound mushrooms, sliced
1 cup hot water
1 cup dry white wine
Dash nutmeg
½ cup tomato paste
1 teaspoon sugar
½ cup cream

Cut veal into 4-inch squares. Mix salt, pepper, and flour, and pound into veal. Brown veal on both sides in combined butter and oil. Remove meat to a warm platter.

Sauté mushrooms in a covered skillet for 10 minutes. Return meat to skillet. Add water, wine, and nutmeg. Cover and simmer 20 minutes or until meat is tender. Add tomato paste, sugar, and cream. Simmer 5 to 10 more minutes. Serves 6 to 8.

Pork Tenderloin Normandy

1   3-pound pork tenderloin
1   tablespoon vegetable oil
1   tablespoon butter
1   medium onion, sliced
1   tart apple, pared, cored
     and sliced
3   tablespoons calvados or 3
     tablespoons apple cider
1   tablespoon all-purpose
     flour
1½ cups veal or chicken stock
Salt and pepper to taste
⅓   cup heavy cream
Watercress

Brown tenderloin on all sides in combined heated oil and butter in a large skillet. Remove meat and set aside.

Add onion to the skillet and cook until tender, but not brown. Add apple slices and continue cooking over medium-high heat until apples and onion are golden.

Replace tenderloin in pan and pour flaming calvados or apple cider over meat. Stir flour into pan juices. Add stock, salt and pepper, and bring to a boil. Cover pan and simmer 40 to 50 minutes, or until meat is tender, stirring occasionally.

Remove tenderloin, carve into ¼-inch diagonal slices and arrange on a platter. Keep warm.

Strain pan sauce, pressing to puree the sliced apple. Bring sauce to a boil and cook to a coating consistency. Add cream to sauce and bring mixture back to a slight boil. Adjust seasonings and spoon over the pork. Garnish with the apple garnish and watercress. Serves 6.

Apple Garnish:
2   tablespoons butter
2   tablespoons sugar
2   firm apples, unpeeled,
     sliced 3/8-inch thick

Heat butter in a skillet. Sprinkle 1 tablespoon sugar over the apple slices. Place slices, sugar side down in the skillet and cook over high heat for 2 or 3 minutes or until sugar is caramelized. Sprinkle remaining 1 tablespoon sugar over apples, turn and cook 2 or 3 more minutes.

Sausage Casserole

2	pounds ground pork sausage
2	onions, chopped
1	green pepper, chopped
1	6-ounce package long grain and wild rice, cooked
1½	cups grated Cheddar cheese
1	10¾-ounce can cream of mushroom soup
¾	cup milk

Brown sausage and onion in a heavy skillet. Add green pepper. Cook 5 minutes and drain fat.

Combine rice, sausage mixture, 1 cup cheese, soup, and milk. Pour into a 2-quart casserole. Sprinkle remaining ½ cup cheese on top. Bake at 350 degrees for 45 minutes. Serves 4 to 6.

Elegant Pork Chops

4	center-cut pork chops, ½ inch thick
½	tablespoon vegetable oil
½	cup apple cider
2	cups veal or beef stock
1	cup heavy cream

Trim fat from chops and slightly pound. Heat oil in a large heavy skillet. Sear pork chops on both sides and remove to a warm platter.

Let skillet cool. Over low heat, pour apple cider into skillet and add 1 cup of the veal or beef stock. Cook until liquid is reduced in half. Slowly add cream to make a thick sauce. If too thick, add some of the remaining stock. Pour sauce over pork chops. Serves 4.

Chinese Spareribs

4	pounds country-style pork spareribs
½	cup soy sauce
¾	cup water
1	12-ounce jar orange marmalade
½	teaspoon garlic powder
½	teaspoon ground ginger

Place ribs in a 12 x 15-inch shallow pan. Bake at 450 degrees for 30 minutes, turning ribs every 10 minutes. Drain excess fat.

Combine soy sauce, water, marmalade, garlic powder, and ginger in a small bowl. Pour sauce over ribs and bake at 350 degrees for 1 hour, turning and basting occasionally. Serves 6 to 8.

Pee Wees

20 small French-style sour
    dough rolls
1   pound ground pork
    sausage
1½ pounds ground chuck
1   large onion, diced
1   egg, beaten
½   cup chopped fresh parsley
2   tablespoons mustard
1   teaspoon salt
1   teaspoon pepper
1   cup grated Parmesan
    cheese
½   teaspoon garlic powder

Slice rolls in half lengthwise. Tear bread out of center of each roll and break into crumbs.

Brown sausage and beef with onion. Drain off any grease. Stir in egg, bread crumbs, parsley, mustard, salt, pepper, and cheese. Cook 10 minutes. Spoon into bottoms of hollowed out rolls. Replace top half of roll over meat mixture to form a sandwich.

Combine butter and garlic powder, and brush each roll with the mixture. Place rolls on a cookie sheet. Bake at 400 degrees for 5 minutes or until brown. Makes 20 sandwiches.

Mom's Turkey Dressing

1   pound lean pork sausage
8   cups corn flakes
1   cup slivered almonds
½   cup chopped celery
½   cup chopped onion
Salt and pepper to taste

Brown sausage in a heavy skillet. Combine corn flakes, almonds, celery, and onion in a large bowl. Add sausage and its grease to the corn flake mixture. Season with salt and pepper, and toss lightly.

Makes enough stuffing for a 12 to 14 pound turkey.

Quick n' Easy Pork Chops

4   center-cut pork chops, 1-
    inch thick
Salt to taste
4   lemon slices
4   tablespoons brown sugar
4   tablespoons catchup

Trim fat from pork chops and place in an ungreased 9 x 12-inch baking pan. Salt chops and top each with a lemon slice. Sprinkle 1 tablespoon brown sugar over each chop and pour 1 tablespoon of catchup over each chop.

Cover and bake at 350 degrees for 1 hour. Uncover and bake 30 more minutes or until all juices have evaporated. Serves 4.

Pork Cutlets à la Crème

6 to 8 pork loin cutlets, ¼-inch
   thick
1   egg
1   tablespoon water
½   cup all-purpose flour
½   teaspoon salt
¼   teaspoon pepper
Butter or margarine
1½ cups half and half
½   cup dry white wine
1   chicken-flavored bouillon
   cube
2   tablespoons minced
   parsley

Pound pork cutlets to about ⅛-inch thick. Cut each into 2 or 3 pieces and set aside.

Beat egg and water with a fork in a pie plate. Combine flour, salt, and pepper. Dip cutlets in egg mixture and then into flour mixture, coating both sides.

Melt 2 tablespoons butter or margarine in a large skillet. Cook cutlet pieces, a few at a time, until brown on both sides, adding more butter as needed. Remove cutlets to a warm platter.

Into the same skillet, over medium heat, stir in half and half, wine, and bouillon, scraping brown bits from bottom of skillet. Cook and stir 3 minutes until thickened and flavors are blended. Pour sauce over cutlets and sprinkle with parsley. Serves 4.

Sausage and Chestnut Stuffing

2   cups chopped onion
½   pound bacon, cut in ½-inch
   pieces
1   pound ground pork
   sausage
Liver from turkey, cooked and
   chopped
2   cups bread cubes, lightly
   toasted
½   cup light cream
2   8-ounce jars chestnuts or
   2-pounds fresh chestnuts,
   cooked and peeled
2   tablespoons sage
2   tablespoons minced, fresh
   parsley
1   teaspoon thyme
½   teaspoon allspice
¼   cup brandy
1   14-pound turkey
Salt and pepper to taste

Sauté onion and bacon in a large heavy skillet until bacon is crisp. With a slotted spoon, transfer bacon and onion to a bowl. Sauté sausage and liver in the remaining fat for 10 minutes or until lightly browned. Using slotted spoon, transfer sausage and liver to the bowl with the bacon mixture.

Soak bread cubes in cream in a small bowl for 10 minutes. Squeeze out excess liquid. Combine bread, meat mixture, chestnuts, and seasonings in a large bowl. Stir in brandy then correct seasonings.

Sprinkle the inside of turkey with salt and pepper, and loosely pack cavities with the stuffing. Spoon remaining stuffing into a buttered 1-quart baking dish. Cover and bake at 325 degrees for 40 minutes. Uncover and bake an additional 20 minutes. Serves 8.

Broiled Oriental Pork

½ **cup soy sauce**
3 **tablespoons sugar**
2 **scallions, chopped**
2 **garlic cloves, minced**
½ **teaspoon pepper**
¼ **teaspoon ginger**
1 **tablespoon sesame seeds**
2 **pounds pork tenderloin, cut ¼-inch thick**
1 **tablespoon peanut oil**

Combine first 7 ingredients in a bowl. Add pork slices and marinate at room temperature for 1 hour, turning meat frequently.

Remove meat from marinade and place on a lightly oiled broiler pan. Broil for 5 minutes on each side or until well browned.

Pour remaining marinade into a saucepan and bring to a boil. Serve with the pork. Serves 4 to 6.

Sausage Stuffed Rigatoni

1 **large onion, finely chopped**
3 **tablespoons olive oil**
2 **6-ounce cans tomato paste**
1 **28-ounce can Italian tomatoes**
4 **cups water**
1 **tablespoon sugar**
1 **teaspoon salt**
½ **teaspoon pepper**
½ **teaspoon oregano**
1 **bay leaf**
2 **pounds ground hot Italian sausage**
¾ **cup Italian-style bread crumbs**
⅓ **cup milk**
2 **eggs**
1 **16-ounce package rigatoni noodles, cooked 5 minutes and drained**
Grated Parmesan cheese

Sauté onion in olive oil. Pour onions, tomato paste, tomatoes, water, and seasonings into a 3-quart saucepan. Stir well; cover and simmer for 1 hour. Remove bay leaf.

Brown sausage and add bread crumbs. Mix milk and eggs together and add to meat mixture. Mix well. Cool.

Stuff each rigatoni with meat mixture. Place a layer of rigatoni in a 4-quart casserole. Pour some of the tomato sauce over noodles and sprinkle with cheese. Repeat layers. Bake at 350 degrees for 1 hour. Serves 10.

Baked Orange Pork Chops

6   center cut pork chops,
    1-inch thick
Salt and pepper to taste
1   cup chopped onion
2   garlic cloves, minced
⅔   cup orange juice
⅔   cup water
3   tablespoons all-purpose
    flour
½   cup water
Parsley for garnish
1   11-ounce can mandarin
    oranges, drained, for
    garnish

Trim excess fat from chops and rub fat on bottom of a heavy skillet to grease. Brown chops on both sides. Remove from skillet and place in a heavy 3-quart casserole. Season with salt and pepper.

Remove excess grease from skillet and lower heat. Add onion and garlic and sauté until lightly browned and tender. Add orange juice and water to pan, and bring to a boil. Add mixture to meat in casserole. Cover dish and bake at 350 degrees for about 2 hours.

Combine flour and water. Slowly stir into juices in the casserole until mixture thickens. Garnish with parsley and oranges. Serves 4.

Spaghetti Primavera

1   tablespoon vegetable oil
1   pound sweet Italian
    sausage
1   28-ounce can Italian plum
    tomatoes
1   cup minced, fresh parsley
2   large garlic cloves, minced
3   red bell peppers, thinly
    sliced
1   teaspoon oregano
3   drops Tabasco
Salt and pepper to taste
1   8-ounce package spaghetti,
    cooked and drained
3   tablespoons minced, fresh
    parsley
3   tablespoons grated
    Parmesan cheese

Heat oil in a large skillet. Add sausage and cook until browned on all sides, about 20 minutes. Remove to a cutting board. To the skillet add tomatoes, parsley, and garlic; bring to a simmer. Add peppers, oregano, Tabasco, salt, and pepper. Cover and simmer gently for 15 minutes.

Thinly slice the sausage and add to the mixture in the skillet. Cover and keep warm. Add spaghetti to skillet and toss thoroughly with the sauce. Sprinkle with parsley and Parmesan cheese. Serves 4 to 6.

Grilled Lamb

1   **7-pound boned leg of
    lamb, butterflied**
13 **ounces white vermouth**
1   **6-ounce can frozen
    lemonade concentrate,
    thawed**
4   **garlic cloves, minced**
½   **teaspoon fresh basil**

Place lamb in a 12 x 15-inch baking dish. Combine vermouth, lemonade, garlic, and basil and pour over lamb. Cover and marinate in the refrigerator for 2 days. Meat will turn a grayish color. Roast meat over very hot coals in a covered grill for 45 minutes. Serves 4 to 6.

Crown Roast of Lamb

1   **5½-pound crown roast of
    lamb, (3 racks tied
    together)**
2   **teaspoons salt**
¼   **teaspoon pepper**
¼   **teaspoon garlic powder**
3   **fresh mint sprigs**
2   **10-ounce packages frozen
    peas, cooked**

Rub meat well with a mixture of salt, pepper, garlic, and mint leaves. Place roast, rib ends down, in a shallow baking pan without a rack. Insert a meat thermometer into center of the fleshy part of meat.

Roast at 300 degrees for 30 minutes. Turn roast once so that the ends are up. Bake another 30 minutes, or until meat thermometer registers 180 degrees. Remove lamb to a platter. Decorate with paper frills. Fill center of roast with peas. Serves 10.

Minted Lamb Chops

6   **loin lamb chops**
Salt and pepper to taste
2   **tablespoons soy sauce**
¼   **cup crème de menthe**

Grease the inside of a pan by rubbing fat edge of a lamp chop over it. Brown chops over high heat 4 to 5 minutes on each side. Drain excess fat. Season with salt and pepper. Add soy sauce and crème de menthe to pan. Stir to blend flavor and spoon over chops. Serves 6.

Braised Lamb Riblets with Green Beans

2   racks of lamb riblets
½   teaspoon salt
½   teaspoon freshly ground pepper
2   garlic cloves, minced
1   tablespoon olive oil
¾   cup chopped onion
1   29-ounce can tomatoes
1   bay leaf
1   pound fresh green beans, or 1 9-ounce package frozen green beans

Cut racks of lamb into 2 sections of 3 ribs. Trim fat and season with salt, pepper, and garlic.

Heat oil in a Dutch oven and brown meat on both sides. Add onion and continue to brown. Drain excess fat. Add tomatoes and bay leaf.

Cover and cook over low heat for 30 minutes. Skim fat. Add green beans and cook for 30 more minutes. Adjust seasonings. Serves 4 to 5.

Lamb Chops in Piquant Sauce

1   tablespoon olive oil
½   teaspoon freshly ground pepper
½   teaspoon oregano
1   garlic clove, minced
8   loin lamb chops, ¾ inch thick
4   anchovy fillets, chopped
2   teaspoons lemon juice
1   tablespoon mustard

Combine oil, pepper, oregano, and garlic. Brush lamb chops with mixture and let stand for 2 hours, basting occasionally.

Mix together anchovies, lemon juice, and mustard and brush onto both sides of chops, reserving ⅓ of mixture. Broil or grill lamb chops for 10 minutes. Turn chops and brush with remaining anchovy mixture. Broil 10 minutes. Serves 4.

POULTRY

Cherry Chicken

1	12-ounce jar cherry preserves
2	tablespoons lemon juice
4	whole cloves
¼	teaspoon salt
¼	teaspoon allspice
¼	teaspoon mace
½	cup all-purpose flour
1	teaspoon salt
1	3-pound chicken or 6 whole chicken breasts, split, boned
¼	cup vegetable oil

Blend first 6 ingredients; set aside. Combine flour and salt and coat chicken. Brown in oil in a skillet at medium heat, turning chicken. Cover and cook 15 minutes. Drain off fat. Add cherry sauce. Cover and simmer over low heat until tender. Turn chicken. Simmer 15 more minutes. Serves 6.

Chicken Livers

6	slices bacon
1	small onion, chopped
1	4-ounce can sliced mushrooms, drained, reserving liquid
1	cup all-purpose flour
½	teaspoon salt
¼	teaspoon pepper
½	teaspoon paprika
1	pound chicken livers
4	tablespoons butter
Sherry	

Cook bacon in a skillet until crisp. Drain and crumble.

Sauté onion in bacon fat until tender. Remove from skillet and drain.

Sauté mushrooms in remaining bacon fat 2 to 3 minutes. Remove and combine with onions and bacon.

Combine flour, salt, pepper, and paprika. Coat chicken livers with mixture.

Melt butter in skillet, add and brown the chicken livers, being careful not to overcook.

Add enough sherry to reserved mushroom liquid to make ½ cup. Pour over livers and simmer 2 to 3 minutes until tender. Add crumbled bacon, onions, and mushrooms, mixing carefully. Serves 3 to 4.

Whole Stuffed Game Hens With Apricot Sauce

⅔ **cup uncooked rice**
3 **teaspoons butter**
1½ **cups boiling water**
½ **cup sliced mushrooms**
2 **teaspoons soy sauce**
1½ **teaspoons salt**
1 **cup diced celery**
1 **teaspoon minced onion**
1 **teaspoon dried parsley flakes**
1 **teaspoon grated orange rind**
½ **teaspoon ground ginger**
½ **teaspoon pepper**
5 to 6 **15-ounce game hens**
1 **teaspoon Accent**
⅛ **teaspoon paprika**

Brown rice in 2 teaspoons butter. Add boiling water and cook 15 minutes or until rice is tender.

Sauté mushrooms in remaining 1 teaspoon butter. Add to rice. Stir in 1 teaspoon soy sauce and 1 teaspoon salt. Add celery, onion, parsley, orange rind, ginger, and ¼ teaspoon pepper.

Rub body and neck cavities of game hens with the remaining 1 teaspoon soy sauce. Fill hens with rice mixture. Lace tightly with strong cord. Rub skin with ½ teaspoon salt, ¼ teaspoon pepper, Accent and paprika. Place hens breast-side up in a 14½ x 10½-inch roasting pan. Bake at 350 degrees for 2 hours, basting with sauce every 20 minutes. Serve with Apricot Sauce. Serves 5 to 6.

Basting Sauce:
¼ **cup hot water**
2 **teaspoons honey**
2 **teaspoons cider vinegar**
2 **teaspoons soy sauce**

Combine ingredients and brush over skin of game hens.

Apricot Sauce:
Giblets and necks from game hens
4 **teaspoons cornstarch**
½ **cup sugar**
1 **8¾-ounce can apricots, drained**
1 **teaspoon soy sauce**

Cover giblets and necks with water in a saucepan. Cook until tender. Reserve 1½ cups broth.

Add cornstarch to a small amount of broth, stirring until smooth. Add sugar, apricots, soy sauce, and remaining broth. Spoon over prepared game hens.

Chicken Curry

5   whole chicken breasts,
    boned and halved
Salt and pepper to taste
1   cup all-purpose flour
6   tablespoons butter
3   apples, finely chopped
2   onions, sliced
2   tablespoons curry powder
Dash ground ginger
3   cups beef broth
1   cup dry white wine
⅓   cup raisins
1   cup heavy cream
6 to 8 cups cooked rice

Season each chicken breast with salt and pepper and dredge chicken in flour. Melt 4 tablespoons butter in a large skillet and sauté chicken until golden brown. Remove chicken.

Melt remaining 2 tablespoons butter in the skillet. Add apples and onion and sauté until soft. Add curry and ginger and cook for 5 minutes. Add beef broth and wine. Add chicken pieces and cover and simmer 1 hour. Stir in raisins and heavy cream. Serve over rice. Serves 8 to 10.

Moo Goo Gai Pien

2   tablespoons cornstarch
½   teaspoon salt
2   whole boneless chicken
    breasts, cut into 1-inch
    cubes
1   tablespoon soy sauce
1   tablespoon sherry
3   tablespoons vegetable oil
2   green onions, sliced
¼   pound fresh mushrooms,
    sliced
½   teaspoon garlic powder
¼   teaspoon ground ginger
1   10¾-ounce can cream of
    chicken soup
1   7-ounce package frozen
    pea pods, thawed
1   7-ounce can water
    chestnuts, drained and
    sliced
3 to 4 cups cooked rice

Combine 1 tablespoon cornstarch and salt in a bowl. Add chicken cubes and coat pieces well. Combine soy sauce, sherry and remaining cornstarch in a separate bowl, blending well. Set aside.

Heat oil in a wok or electric skillet to 375 degrees. Add chicken pieces and cook, stirring constantly, 2 to 3 minutes. Remove chicken and add onion and mushrooms to the pan. Add garlic powder and ginger. Cook, stirring constantly for 1 minute. Stir in chicken soup. Gradually add soy sauce mixture, stirring constantly until thick. Add pea pods, water chestnuts, and chicken. Cook until heated. Serve over rice. Serves 4.

Chinese Chicken with Nuts

1 egg white
1 tablespoon soy sauce
¼ teaspoon salt
1 tablespoon cornstarch
1 pound boneless chicken breasts, cut into small cubes
1 cup vegetable oil
⅔ cup unsalted cashews, peanuts or walnuts
1 small slice fresh ginger
2 green onions, sliced
1 green pepper, cut into small cubes
1 8-ounce can water chestnuts, drained and sliced
4 cups cooked rice

Combine egg white, soy sauce, salt, and cornstarch in a large bowl. Add chicken cubes and marinate for 30 minutes.

Heat oil in a large skillet or wok. Deep fry the nuts over medium heat to a light brown, about 1 to 2 minutes. Remove nuts and drain. Add chicken and stir-fry 1 to 2 minutes until meat turns white. Remove chicken.

Discard all but 2 tablespoons oil from pan. Add ginger, onion, pepper, and water chestnuts and stir-fry for 1 minute. Add chicken and seasoning sauce and stir until sauce thickens. Discard the ginger and add nuts. Serve over rice. Serves 6.

Seasoning Sauce:
2½ tablespoons soy sauce
½ tablespoon vinegar
1 tablespoon sherry
1 teaspoon sugar
1 teaspoon cornstarch

Combine all ingredients in a bowl.

Marinated Cornish Hens

½ cup vegetable oil
1 teaspoon ground oregano
½ teaspoon garlic salt
4 Cornish hens
½ cup all-purpose flour
1 teaspoon salt
1 teaspoon pepper
1 cup water
½ cup sherry
Paprika to taste

Combine oil, ½ teaspoon oregano, and garlic salt. Pour over hens and marinate in refrigerator overnight, turning several times. Drain.

Tie legs of hens together and roll in flour seasoned with salt and pepper. Brown in oil in a large Dutch oven. Add water, sherry, remaining oregano, and paprika. Cover and bake at 350 degrees for 1½ hours.

Livers and gizzards may be cooked separately until tender. Chop and add to gravy before serving. Serves 4.

Overnight Chicken

1   cup sour cream
1   garlic clove, pressed
1   teaspoon celery salt
1   teaspoon salt
2   tablespoons lemon juice
1   teaspoon Worcestershire
    sauce
Pepper to taste
Paprika to taste
½   cup bread crumbs
½   cup butter

Combine the first 8 ingredients in a bowl. Coat chicken breasts with mixture and place in a buttered 2-quart baking dish and marinate overnight.

Sprinkle with bread crumbs and place a pat of butter on each breast. Bake uncovered at 350 degrees for 1 hour and 15 minutes. Serves 4 to 6.

Chicken Spaghetti

2   large chickens or 4 whole
    breasts
2   quarts water
Onion, celery salt, pepper to
    taste
1   16-ounce package
    vermicelli
½   cup butter
2   large onions, chopped
2   large green peppers,
    seeded, chopped
1   10-ounce can tomatoes
2   tablespoons
    Worcestershire sauce
1   pound processed cheese,
    chopped
1   8½-ounce can tiny peas,
    drained
1   4-ounce can button
    mushrooms, drained
Salt and pepper to taste

Cook chicken in water which has been seasoned with onion, celery salt, and pepper until chicken is tender. Reserve 1½-quarts broth. Chop chicken.

Cook vermicelli in chicken broth. Drain.

Melt butter in a skillet. Add onion and pepper and sauté until tender. Add tomatoes and Worcestershire sauce. Cook until thickened. Stir in cheese until melted. Add peas, mushrooms, chicken, and vermicelli. Pour into a 3-quart casserole. Bake at 350 degrees for 30 minutes. Serves 8 to 10.

Tarragon Chicken Surprise

2   tablespoons all-purpose
     flour
1   cup chicken broth
4   half chicken breasts,
     boned, skinned, cut into
     bite-size pieces
2   teaspoons salt
¼   cup vegetable oil
1   small onion, chopped
1   bay leaf
1   cup whole fresh
     mushrooms
½   cup chopped, fresh parsley
¼   cup chopped walnuts
1¼   teaspoons tarragon
½   teaspoon pepper
1   cup sour cream
1   8-ounce package noodles,
     cooked

Combine flour with ¼ cup of broth in a small bowl, stirring until smooth.

Sprinkle chicken with salt. Heat oil in a skillet, add onion and sauté about 3 minutes over medium heat. Add chicken and cook about 10 minutes, turning chicken until brown on all sides. Drain chicken.

Remove oil from skillet. Pour ¾ cup broth into skillet. Add flour mixture and cook, stirring, over medium heat about 5 minutes or until thick.

Add bay leaf and chicken pieces. Cover and simmer 25 minutes or until tender. Add mushrooms, parsley, walnuts, tarragon, and pepper. Cook uncovered 10 minutes. Remove from heat and stir in sour cream. Serve with noodles. Serves 4.

Marinated Chicken

2   chickens, cup up
Seasoned salt, pepper, and
     lemon juice to taste

Sprinkle chicken pieces with seasoned salt, pepper, and lemon juice. Place chicken in a container and pour marinade sauce over chicken. Cover and marinate overnight in refrigerator. Grill over low heat for 45 to 60 minutes, basting frequently with sauce. Serves 8.

Marinade Sauce:
2   cups butter or margarine
1   5-ounce jar horseradish
Juice of 6 lemons
3   tablespoons
     Worcestershire sauce
2   tablespoons Tabasco
1   cup vinegar

Combine and heat all ingredients in a saucepan, stirring well to blend. Cool. Makes 5 cups.

Chicken Tetrazzini

1   chicken or 6 to 8 half
    breasts
1   teaspoon salt
2   quarts water
1   10-ounce package noodles
1   cup butter
1   medium green pepper,
    chopped
1   medium onion, minced
1   pound fresh mushrooms,
    sliced
⅔   cup all-purpose flour
2   cups milk
2   cups grated American
    cheese
2   cups grated Cheddar
    cheese
1   8-ounce jar processed
    cheese spread
Salt and pepper to taste
Worcestershire sauce, garlic
    salt, seasoned salt, and
    Tabasco to taste
Paprika

Cook chicken in salted water until tender. Remove from broth, cool, bone, and cut into bite-size pieces. Strain broth, removing fat. Cook noodles in 1 quart chicken broth.

Melt butter in a saucepan. Add green pepper, onion, and mushrooms and cook until tender. Add flour and blend well. Add milk and 2 cups of the chicken broth and cook until sauce is thickened. Stir in cheeses and cook over low heat until melted.

Combine chicken, noodles, and cheese sauce. Add seasonings to taste. Pour into a 3-quart casserole.

Sprinkle paprika on top. Bake at 350 degrees for 40 minutes. Serves 10 to 12.

Virginia's Chicken

1   chicken, cut-up
Salt and pepper to taste
1   cup butter, melted
¼   teaspoon basil
¼   teaspoon rosemary
½   cup chopped onion
1   10¾-ounce can cream of
    mushroom soup

Season chicken with salt and pepper and place in a 2-quart shallow baking dish. Combine remaining ingredients and pour over chicken. Bake uncovered at 350 degrees for 1½ hours. Serves 4 to 6.

Hot Chicken Salad

3   cups chopped, cooked
     chicken
1   cup chopped celery
3   hard-cooked eggs, chopped
½   cup water chestnuts,
     drained and sliced
½   cup mayonnaise
1   tablespoon lemon juice
1   10¾-ounce can cream of
     chicken soup
½   teaspoon salt
½   teaspoon pepper
½   teaspoon Worcestershire
     sauce
½   cup Parmesan cheese

Combine all ingredients, except Parmesan cheese, in a large bowl. Pour into a 2-quart casserole or individual ramekins and top with cheese. Bake at 400 degrees for 20 minutes. Serves 6 to 8.

Chicken-Shrimp Supreme

½   pound mushrooms, sliced
2   tablespoons sliced green
     onion
¼   cup butter, melted
2   10¾-ounce cans cream of
     chicken soup
½   cup sherry
½   cup light cream
1   cup shredded Cheddar
     cheese
2   cups diced cooked chicken
2   cups cooked shrimp,
     shelled and deveined
2   tablespoons chopped
     parsley
1   10-ounce package frozen
     patty shells, baked

Combine mushrooms and onion with butter in a 3-quart saucepan and sauté for 5 minutes. Add soup and gradually stir in sherry and cream. Add cheese and heat over low heat, stirring occasionally until cheese is melted. Add chicken and shrimp. Heat, but do not boil. Add parsley at last minute. Serve in patty shells. Serves 4 to 6.

Mildred's Chicken Casserole

3   cups cooked, diced chicken
     breasts
1   6-ounce box wild and herb
     rice
2   10¾-ounce cans cream of
     celery soup
1   2-ounce jar chopped
     pimento
1½ cups mayonnaise
1   8-ounce can sliced water
     chestnuts, drained
1   14-ounce can artichoke
     hearts, drained
Salt and pepper to taste
3   tablespoons soy sauce
½   cup packaged dry stuffing

Combine all ingredients, except stuffing, and pour into a 3-quart casserole. Sprinkle stuffing on top. Bake at 350 degrees for 30 to 40 minutes until bubbly. Serves 6 to 8.

Chicken From the Tropics

2   chickens, cut up
1   teaspoon salt
1   teaspoon pepper
1   cup all-purpose flour
1   teaspoon paprika
½   cup vegetable oil
½   cup butter, melted
1   30-ounce can sliced
     pineapple
4   to 5 sliced green onions
     and tops
1   green pepper, seeded, cut
     in strips
½   cup dry white wine
1   tablespoon brown sugar
Dash salt
½   cup diced almonds

Season chicken with salt and pepper. Coat chicken with flour and season with paprika. Combine oil and butter in a bowl and turn chicken in mixture until completely coated. Place chicken skin-side down in a single layer in a 9 x 13-inch baking dish. Bake at 400 degrees for 30 minutes. Turn chicken.

Cut ½ of pineapple slices into bite-size pieces. Cut remaining pineapple into half-slices. Combine pineapple with syrup, onions, green pepper, wine, brown sugar, and salt. Pour mixture over and around chicken. Sprinkle with almonds. Bake at 375 degrees about 45 minutes basting occasionally. Serves 8.

Chicken Provencal

½ cup all-purpose flour
½ teaspoon salt
¼ teaspoon pepper
1 chicken, cut-up
¼ cup olive oil
2 chicken bouillon cubes
1 cup boiling water
½ cup chopped green pepper
12 small white onions, peeled
¼ cup chopped green onions
3 garlic cloves, minced
2 tablespoons parsley
½ cup dry white wine
2 teaspoons salt
¼ teaspoon pepper
1 bay leaf
6 medium tomatoes, peeled seeded, cut into strips
½ cup halved black olives
¼ teaspoon thyme
¼ teaspoon Tabasco
1 2-ounce jar pimentos, drained
1 4-ounce can sliced mushrooms, drained
2 tablespoons parsley

Combine flour, ½ teaspoon salt and ¼ teaspoon pepper, and roll chicken in seasoned mixture. In a large skillet, slowly brown chicken in oil over medium heat.

While chicken browns, dissolve bouillon cubes in boiling water and set aside. Place browned chicken pieces in a 2-quart casserole.

Drain off oil in the skillet except for 1 tablespoon. In oil, sauté green pepper, onions, green onions, and garlic for 5 minutes. Add 2 tablespoons salt, ¼ teaspoon pepper, and remaining ingredients, except parsley. Simmer at low heat for 5 minutes.

Pour sauce over chicken. Cover and bake at 350 degrees for 45 minutes. Remove bay leaf. Garnish with parsley. Serves 4 to 6.

Chicken Casserole

1　10¾-ounce can cream of celery soup
1　10¾-ounce can cream of chicken soup
½　cup mayonnaise
½　teaspoon salt
½　teaspoon pepper
1　teaspoon Worcestershire sauce
Dash garlic salt
5　drops Tabasco
5　cups cooked, diced chicken breasts
2　cups dry, packaged herb stuffing
1　cup cornflake crumbs, buttered
¼　cup slivered almonds

Combine celery and chicken soups together in a bowl.

Layer chicken, stuffing, and soup mixture in a 3-quart baking dish. Repeat layers. Top with cornflake crumbs and sprinkle with slivered almonds. Bake at 350 degrees for 30 to 45 minutes until bubbly. Serves 6.

Indonesian Chicken

1　medium onion, chopped
¼　cup butter or margarine
2　small bay leaves
1½ teaspoons tumeric
1½ teaspoons paprika
1　teaspoon cinnamon
½　teaspoon cumin
½　teaspoon garlic salt
1　teaspoon sugar
Dash cayenne
6　half chicken breasts
1　cup tomato puree
1½ cups canned tomatoes, drained
½　cup white wine

Sauté onion with butter and bay leaves in a skillet until golden brown. Add all seasonings and cook 3 minutes. Add chicken breasts and sauté for 10 minutes. Add tomato puree and tomatoes and cook 10 more minutes. Add wine. Pour into a 2-quart baking dish and bake covered at 350 degrees for 45 minutes. Uncover and bake an additional 15 minutes. Serves 6.

Mexican Chicken Casserole

1   3 to 4-pound chicken or 6
    half breasts
1   onion
2   celery stalks
Salt and pepper to taste
1   10¾-ounce can cream of
    mushroom soup
1   10¾-ounce can cream of
    chicken soup
½   pound Cheddar cheese,
    grated
12 corn tortillas
2   onions, chopped
1   large green pepper, seeded,
    chopped
¾   teaspoon chili powder
½   teaspoon garlic salt
1   teaspoon Worcestershire
    sauce
1   10-ounce can tomatoes
    with chilies

Boil chicken 30 minutes, or until tender, in water seasoned with 1 onion, 2 stalks celery, salt, and pepper. Cut chicken into bite-size pieces and reserve stock.

Combine soups and cheese.

Soak tortillas in boiling stock until dripping with stock.

Layer half of tortillas, chicken, onion, green pepper, chili powder, garlic salt, Worcestershire sauce, and cheese mixture in a 9 x 12-inch baking dish. Repeat the layers. Pour tomatoes with chilies and juices over casserole. Bake uncovered at 375 degrees for 30 minutes. This should be made at least one day in advance for flavors to blend. Serves 8 to 10.

Poppy Seed Chicken

12 half chicken breasts,
   cooked boned, seasoned,
   torn into pieces
2   10¾-ounce cans cream of
    chicken soup
1   cup sour cream
½   cup sherry
Dash salt and pepper
½   teaspoon lemon pepper
2   tablespoons
    Worcestershire sauce
35 to 40 butter-flavored
   crackers, crumbled
2   tablespoons poppy seeds
6   tablespoons butter, melted

Combine chicken, soup, sour cream, sherry and seasonings. Pour into a 3-quart casserole.

Combine crackers, poppy seeds and butter and top casserole with mixture. Bake at 350 degrees for 30 minutes. Serves 10.

Ham Stuffed Chicken Breasts

½   pound fresh mushrooms, sliced
8   tablespoons butter
6   half chicken breasts, skinned, boned
6   thin slices ham
6   slices Swiss cheese
6   tablespoons all-purpose flour
1   teaspoon salt
1   teaspoon pepper
1   tablespoon vegetable oil
1   cup chicken stock, heated
¼   cup dry, white wine
Dash Tabasco
Dash Worcestershire sauce
¼   cup slivered almonds, toasted

Sauté mushrooms with 1 tablespoon butter in a small pan. Set aside.

Pound chicken breasts to about ¼-inch thickness. Place a slice of ham and a slice of cheese on each breast. Roll up lengthwise and secure with toothpicks. Mix flour, ½ teaspoon salt and ½ teaspoon pepper. Coat rolled chicken breasts in flour. Reserve seasoned flour.

In a large skillet, heat 4 tablespoons butter and the oil and brown chicken rolls. Arrange chicken in 1 layer in a greased, shallow 2-quart casserole.

Discard remaining butter and oil from skillet and melt the remaining 3 tablespoons butter. Add 2 tablespoons of seasoned flour and cook over medium heat, stirring constantly until light brown. Slowly add chicken stock, stirring constantly until smooth. Add wine, ½ teaspoon salt, ¼ teaspoon pepper, Tabasco, Worcestershire sauce, and sautéed mushrooms. Simmer over low heat for 5 minutes and pour over chicken. Cover and bake at 350 degrees for 30 minutes. Garnish with toasted almonds. Serves 6.

Chicken Gourmet

4	**whole chicken breasts, boned**
¼	**cup butter**
1	**teaspoon salt**
¼	**teaspoon paprika**
¼	**teaspoon pepper**
1	**6-ounce package long grain and wild rice, cooked**

Parsley

Baste breasts, inside and out, with butter, salt, paprika, and pepper. Spoon rice into breasts and skewer shut. Place in a 9 x 13-inch baking dish and bake uncovered at 350 degrees for 1½ hours, basting every 15 minutes with melting butter.

Serve on a platter, garnished with parsley. Pass sauce separately. Serves 4.

Sauce:

¼	**cup dry white wine**
¼	**cup currant jelly**
1	**10¾-ounce can cream of mushroom soup**
½	**teaspoon Tabasco**
¼	**cup chopped onion**
½	**pound mushrooms, sliced**
2	**tablespoons butter**

Slowly heat wine, jelly, soup, and Tabasco in a saucepan.

Sauté onion and mushrooms in butter, in a separate pan. Combine with sauce and heat. Do not boil.

Chicken Oyster Bake

1	**3-pound chicken, cut up**
2	**tablespoons oil**
2	**tablespoons chopped onion**
1	**garlic clove, minced**
½	**cup water**
½	**cup sherry**
1	**4-ounce can sliced mushrooms and liquid**
½	**teaspoon pepper**
1	**tablespoon Worcestershire sauce**
1	**10¾-ounce can cream of mushroom soup**
1	**pint oysters and liquid**

3 to 4 cups cooked rice

Brown chicken in oil in a skillet. Transfer pieces to shallow 2-quart casserole.

Sauté onion and garlic in pan drippings. Remove from heat and stir in water, sherry, mushrooms, pepper, Worcestershire sauce, and soup. Pour over chicken. Cover and bake at 350 degrees for 45 minutes. Uncover and stir in oysters. Bake 15 minutes more. Serve over rice. Serves 4 to 6.

Coq au Vin

1 **4-pound chicken, cut up**
3 **tablespoons butter**
¾ **cup chopped onion**
2 **carrots, sliced**
3 **shallots, minced**
2 **tablespoons all-purpose flour**
1 **chicken bouillon cube**
3 **tablespoons minced parsley**
1 **teaspoon marjoram**
⅛ **teaspoon thyme**
½ **bay leaf**
1 **teaspoon salt**
¼ **teaspoon black pepper**
2 **tablespoons brandy**
1 **teaspoon Worcestershire sauce**
Dash Tabasco
1 **cup dry white wine**
½ **pound mushrooms, sliced**

Brown chicken in butter. Add next 6 ingredients and brown lightly. Push vegetables aside and stir in remaining ingredients, except wine and mushrooms. When mixture is blended, add wine and cover. Simmer chicken over low heat until done, about 1 hour. Add mushrooms. Cover and cook 15 more minutes. Skim off excess fat. Serve chicken on a platter covered with the vegetables and sauce. Serves 6.

Chicken Divan

12 **half chicken breasts, boned**
¾ **cup butter**
½ **cup all-purpose flour**
3 **cups chicken broth**
3 **egg yolks**
1 **cup heavy cream, whipped**
2 **tablespoons dry white wine or sherry**
Salt and pepper to taste
2 **bunches broccoli, cooked, drained**
1 **cup grated, fresh Parmesan cheese**

Sauté chicken breasts for 20 minutes in ¼ cup butter.

Melt ½ cup butter in a large saucepan and stir in flour. Add chicken broth, stirring constantly until mixture comes to a boil. Simmer about 5 minutes. Cool slightly. Beat in egg yolks. Fold in whipped cream along with wine or sherry. Season with salt and pepper.

Place broccoli in a 3-quart baking dish. Cover broccoli with ½ of sauce. Cover sauce with ½ of the cheese. Arrange browned chicken breasts on top of cheese. Top with remaining sauce and cheese. Bake at 350 degrees for 20 minutes. Freezes well. Serves 10 to 12.

Chicken Cacciatore

1	3 to 4-pound chicken, cut-up

Salt and pepper to taste

¼	cup olive oil
2	medium onions, chopped
1	garlic clove, minced
½	cup white wine

Cooked rice or noodles

¼	cup chopped parsley

Season chicken with salt and pepper and brown in oil. Remove chicken from skillet and sauté onions and garlic until tender, but not brown. Return chicken to skillet and pour sauce over chicken. Simmer for 1 hour. Add wine and simmer, covered, for 15 minutes. Serve over hot rice or buttered noodles. Garnish with parsley. Serves 6.

Sauce:

1	16-ounce can tomatoes
1	8-ounce can seasoned tomato sauce
1	teaspoon salt
½	teaspoon pepper
½	teaspoon celery salt
1	teaspoon oregano
1	teaspoon Worcestershire sauce

Dash Tabasco

Combine all ingredients in a bowl.

French Chicken

12	half chicken breasts
2	tablespoons butter
2	14-ounce cans artichoke hearts, drained
1	6-ounce can pitted black olives, drained
⅓	cup white wine
2	chicken bouillon cubes, dissolved in 1 cup boiling water

Salt and pepper to taste
Dash Worcestershire sauce
Dash Tabasco

¼	cup chopped parsley
1	16-ounce package linguine, cooked

Brown chicken in butter in a skillet. Place chicken in a large dutch oven. Add remaining ingredients, except linguine. Cover and simmer about 1½ hours. Serve over linguine.
Serves 8 to 12.

Turkey Mornay

1 cup chopped green onion
½ cup butter
¾ cup all-purpose flour
½ to 1 cup milk
¼ cup grated, fresh Parmesan cheese
1 cup grated, mild Cheddar cheese
½ teaspoon salt
½ teaspoon pepper
1 teaspoon Worcestershire sauce
½ teaspoon garlic salt
½ cup chopped, fresh parsley
1 8-ounce package frozen asparagus, cooked
12 slices turkey
Paprika

Sauté onion with butter in a saucepan until tender. Stir in flour. Slowly stir in milk to make a thick white sauce. Add cheese and stir until melted. Add seasonings.

Place asparagus spears in bottom of a greased 2-quart casserole. Place turkey slices on top and pour sauce over turkey. Sprinkle liberally with paprika. Bake at 350 degrees for about 20 minutes until hot and bubbly. This may also be prepared in individual shells. Serves 8.

Chicken Tetrazzini

½ pound mushrooms
1 cup butter
2 tablespoons all-purpose flour
2 cups chicken broth
1 cup heavy cream
¼ cup sherry
2 cups grated, fresh Parmesan cheese
Salt to taste
Dash cayenne
4 half chicken breasts, cooked, diced
1 8-ounce package spaghetti, cooked

Sauté mushrooms in a saucepan in 1 tablespoon butter. Remove mushrooms and add remaining butter and flour to pan. Slowly stir in broth. Add cream and sherry. Add cheese, salt, and pepper.

Combine sauce with mushrooms, diced chicken, and spaghetti. Bake in a 2-quart casserole at 350 degrees for 30 to 40 minutes until bubbly.

Serves 6 to 8.

Parisian Chicken

6   half chicken breasts
1   teaspoon salt
½   teaspoon pepper
½   cup butter
2   tablespoons brandy
2   tomatoes, peeled, diced
3   shallots, finely chopped
½   teaspoon paprika
1   teaspoon Worcestershire
    sauce
1   cup dry white wine
½   teaspoon tarragon
3   tablespoons heavy cream
Kitchen Bouquet

Season breasts with salt and pepper and brown slowly in butter, in a dutch oven. Dissolve pan juices with brandy. Add next 6 ingredients. Simmer 30 minutes or until chicken is tender. Stir in cream and add a few drops of Kitchen Bouquet for color. Serves 4 to 6.

Chicken Vol-au-Vent

6   chicken thighs
2   tablespoons butter
1   chicken bouillon cube
½   cup water
3   tablespoons all-purpose
    flour
¼   teaspoon paprika
¼   teaspoon salt
Dash pepper
1   cup light cream
1   6-ounce jar sliced
    mushrooms, drained
¼   cup white wine
6   brown-and-serve sausages,
    cooked
1   10-ounce package frozen
    patty shells, thawed
1   egg yolk
2   tablespoons light cream

Brown chicken in butter. Dissolve bouillon in water and add to chicken. Cover and simmer 30 minutes until tender. Remove chicken and cool. Carefully remove bones and skin from chicken. Measure broth and add water to make 1 cup. Return to skillet.

Combine flour, paprika, salt, and pepper. Stir in 1 cup cream and add to chicken broth. Cook until thickened. Stir in mushrooms and wine.

Place a sausage in bone cavity of each thigh. Roll each patty shell into a 6-inch square on a lightly floured surface. Place thigh in center of pastry and top with 2 tablespoons of cream sauce. Fold pastry over and seal. Fold ends to center and seal. Place seam-side down on a greased baking sheet.

Combine egg yolk and 2 tablespoons light cream and brush over pastry. Bake at 400 degrees for 30 minutes. Heat remaining sauce and serve with chicken. Serves 6.

Chicken and Broccoli

3   tablespoons chopped onion
1   green pepper, seeded,
     chopped
3   tablespoons butter
6 to 8 half chicken breasts,
     cooked, boned, cut into
     pieces
4   10-ounce packages frozen
     broccoli, cooked
1   10¾-ounce can cream of
     mushroom soup
1   10¾-ounce can cream of
     chicken soup
2   6-ounce packages garlic
     cheese
2   cups sour cream
1   8-ounce can mushrooms,
     drained
2   teaspoons Worcestershire
     sauce
¼   teaspoon Tabasco
Salt and pepper to taste
½   cup bread crumbs

Sauté onion and green pepper in butter until tender. Combine with remaining ingredients, except bread crumbs, in a large bowl. Pour into a 3-quart casserole. Top with bread crumbs. Bake at 350 degrees for 30 minutes until bubbly. Serves 8 to 10.

CHEESE & EGGS

Blackbird Quiche

1¼ cups milk
3   eggs
1   tablespoon all-purpose
    flour
4   ounces Swiss cheese,
    grated
2   ounces Cheddar cheese,
    grated
4   scallions, chopped
4   tablespoons chopped black
    olives
1   cup chopped meat or
    vegetables, optional
1   baked 9-inch pie shell

Beat together milk, eggs and flour. Add cheese, scallions, and olives. Stir in meats or vegetables, if desired. Pour into pie shell and bake at 350 degrees for 1 hour, or until firm. Serves 4 to 6.

Brunch Casserole

¼   cup butter
16 slices bread, crusts
    removed
8   slices ham
8   slices sharp Cheddar
    cheese
6   eggs beaten
½   teaspoon salt
Dash pepper
¾   teaspoon dry mustard
¼   cup minced onion
¼   cup finely chopped green
    pepper
2   teaspoons Worcestershire
    sauce
⅛   teaspoon garlic powder
½   teaspoon oregano
3   cups milk
Dash red pepper
½   cup butter, melted
1   cup crushed potato chips,

Butter both sides of bread. Layer 8 slices of bread in a 9 x 13-inch baking dish. Place 1 slice ham on top of each slice of bread. Place cheese on top of ham. Place remaining bread on top of cheese.

Combine the next 11 ingredients and pour over casserole. Cover and let stand overnight.

Pour melted butter over casserole. Top with crushed potato chips. Bake at 350 degrees for 1 hour. Serves 8.

Asparagus Omelet

Omelet:
3   eggs
3   teaspoons water
Dash salt
3   drops Tabasco
1 to 1¼ tablespoons butter
6   asparagus spears, cooked

Break eggs into a small bowl. Add water, salt, and Tabasco. Beat with a fork until whites and yolks are just blended.

Melt butter in an omelet pan or skillet over moderately high heat. Pour ⅓ of egg mixture into pan. When omelet has set on the bottom, tilt pan and lift edge of omelet to allow uncooked egg, on top, to flow under cooked portion. Cook longer, until slightly brown on the outside, but still creamy. Remove from pan to serving plate.

Place 2 asparagus spears and some sauce in omelet before folding. Spoon some sauce over top. Repeat procedure to make 2 more omelets. Serves 3.

Asparagus Sauce:
2   tablespoons butter
2   tablespoons all-purpose flour
1   cup milk
½   teaspoon salt
½   teaspoon celery salt
¼   teaspoon white pepper
½   cup grated Parmesan cheese
1   hard-cooked egg, chopped
4   asparagus spears, cooked

Melt butter in a saucepan. Stir in flour and cook 2 minutes. Gradually add milk. Cook, stirring, over low heat until sauce thickens. Stir in salt, celery salt, pepper, cheese, and egg. Cut asparagus spears into small pieces. Stir pieces into sauce.

Eggs Louis

½   cup packaged seasoned croutons, crushed
¾   cup grated sharp cheese
2   eggs
Butter or margarine

Sprinkle ⅓ of the crouton crumbs evenly over bottom of a buttered single serving casserole. Sprinkle ½ of the cheese over croutons.

Carefully break eggs over the cheese. Sprinkle remaining crumbs and cheese over eggs. Dot with butter. Bake at 325 degrees for 15 to 20 minutes. Serves 1.

Early Morning French Toast

12 eggs
2   cups small-curd cottage
    cheese
1   tablespoon cinnamon
1   teaspoon vanilla
6   slices raisin bread
Syrup or jam

Combine eggs in a blender or processor, blending 5 to 10 seconds until well beaten. Add cottage cheese, cinnamon, and vanilla and blend for 8 seconds.

Place bread slices, in a single layer, in a greased 9 x 13-inch baking dish. Pour egg mixture over bread. Cover and refrigerate overnight. Bake at 350 degrees for 30 to 40 minutes or until set. Cut into squares and serve with syrup or jam. Serves 6.

Continental French Toast

8   slices French bread, ¾-inch
    thick
4   eggs, beaten
1   cup milk
2   tablespoons Cointreau or
    Grand Marnier
1   tablespoon sugar
½   teaspoon vanilla
¼   teaspoon salt
2   tablespoons butter
Confectioners' sugar
Syrup

Arrange bread in a flat 9 x 11-inch baking dish. Combine eggs, milk, Cointreau, sugar, vanilla, and salt. Pour mixture over bread. Cover dish and refrigerate overnight.

Melt butter in a skillet. Sauté each bread slice for 4 minutes on each side. Sprinkle with confectioners' sugar. Serve with syrup. Serves 6 to 8.

Brunch Eggs

2   10¾-ounce cans cream of
    mushroom soup
½   cup sherry
1   4-ounce can mushrooms,
    drained
3   dozen eggs
¼   cup milk
½   cup butter
½   pound grated Cheddar
    cheese
Paprika to taste

Heat soup just enough to stir smooth. Add sherry and mushrooms.

Beat eggs and milk together. Melt butter in a pan and scramble egg mixture until just soft.

Pour a layer of eggs into a casserole. Add a layer of soup mixture and a layer of cheese. Repeat. Sprinkle with paprika. Place dish into a cold oven and turn temperature to 250 degrees. Bake for 1 hour, or until thoroughly heated. Serves 12 to 14.

Egg Casserole

¾ pound sharp Cheddar
    cheese, sliced ¼-inch thick
1   teaspoon dry mustard
1   teaspoon paprika
1¼ teaspoons salt
1   cup sour cream
1   pound mild, ground
    sausage, cooked
10 eggs

Cover bottom of a 9 x 13-inch casserole with ½ of the cheese slices. Mix seasonings with sour cream, and pour ½ of mixture over cheese. Sprinkle on sausage. Place remaining cheese over sausage.

Break eggs over cheese and cover eggs with remaining sour cream mixture. Bake at 325 degrees for 15 to 20 minutes or until eggs are set. Serves 6 to 8.

Frittata Provencal

Frittata:
4   eggs
Dash salt and pepper
½   cup grated sharp cheese
2   tablespoons olive oil

Combine provencal filling with eggs, salt, pepper, and cheese, mixing well.

Heat oil in a 7 or 8-inch oven-proof skillet. Pour egg mixture into heated pan, and cook eggs until partially set.

Place skillet under broiler, as far away from heat as possible, and broil eggs for 5 to 10 minutes, or until top is set and lightly browned. Slide eggs out of pan onto a plate lined with paper towel to blot moisture. Cut into wedges. Serves 2 to 3.

Provencal Filling:
2   tablespoons olive oil
6 to 8 fresh mushrooms, sliced
1   large onion, chopped
½   green pepper, chopped
2   zucchini, thinly sliced
½   eggplant, diced
3   tomatoes, peeled, seeded
    and chopped
1   garlic clove, minced
½   teaspoon sweet basil
Dash salt and pepper
3   tablespoons grated
    Parmesan cheese

Heat oil in a large skillet. Sauté mushrooms over high heat 2 to 3 minutes. Remove from pan and reserve. Add onions to skillet and sauté 5 minutes until tender. Add green pepper, zucchini and eggplant and cook 5 minutes.

Add tomatoes and seasonings, except for cheese. Cover and cook over low heat for 10 to 15 minutes. Add mushrooms and cook, uncovered, another 10 minutes or until mixture is fairly dry. Stir in cheese. Remove from heat.

Breakfast Soufflé

12 slices firm bread, toasted,
    crusts removed
1   pound Canadian bacon,
    sliced
6   ounces Swiss cheese,
    grated
4   eggs
1   teaspoon salt
½   teaspoon pepper
¼   teaspoon nutmeg
3   cups milk
2   tablespoons butter

Spread slices of toast with hollandaise butter. Line buttom of a greased 9 x 13-inch ovenproof dish with 6 slices of toast.

Layer ½ of the bacon, and then sprinkle ½ of the cheese over toast. Repeat bacon and cheese. Top with remaining 6 slices of buttered toast.

Place eggs and seasonings in a blender and blend well. Add 1 cup milk and blend. Add mixture to the remaining 2 cups milk and stir. Pour mixture over bread. Cover and refrigerate 3 to 4 hours or overnight. Dot with butter. Bake at 350 degrees for 45 minutes or until set. Serves 8.

Hollandaise Butter:
½   cup unsalted butter,
    softened
3   egg yolks
½   teaspoon salt
Dash cayenne
Juice of 1 lemon
1   teaspoon very hot water

Combine first 5 ingredients. Add water and mix well.

Salmon Soufflé Quiche

1   7¾-ounce can salmon,
    drained, liquid reserved
1   unbaked 9-inch pie shell
2   tablespoons chopped green
    onion
2   3-ounce packages cream
    cheese, softened
2   tablespoons lemon juice
¼   teaspoon salt
4   eggs, separated
Pimento for garnish

Spread salmon chunks over bottom of pie shell. Cover salmon with chopped onion.

Combine cream cheese and lemon juice. Gradually beat in salmon liquid, salt, and cream. Beat egg yolks lightly, and stir into cheese mixture.

Beat egg whites until stiff, and gently fold into cheese mixture. Spoon over salmon. Bake at 375 degrees for 45 minutes, or until filling is set. Garnish with pimento. Cut into wedges. Serves 6.

Baked Chilies Retaloes

6   eggs, separated
1   tablespoon all-purpose
    flour
¼   teaspoon salt
⅛   teaspoon pepper
1   4-ounce can chili peppers,
    drained
8   ounces Monterey Jack
    cheese, grated

Beat egg whites until stiff. Mix together flour, salt, pepper and egg yolks. Fold mixture into egg whites. Pour ½ of the mixture into a greased 7 x 13-inch baking dish.

Remove stubs from chilies and chop. Spread chilies over egg mixture and cover with grated cheese. Pour remaining egg mixture over cheese. Bake at 325 degrees for 25 minutes. Cut into 3-inch squares. Serve with bottled hot sauce. Serves 6 to 8.

Old English Spinach Soufflé

1   12-ounce carton small-
    curd cottage cheese
6   eggs
6   tablespoons all-purpose
    flour
1   10-ounce package frozen
    chopped spinach, thawed
    and drained
½   cup butter or margarine,
    melted
12 slices Old English cheese,
    diced
2   teaspoons salt

Combine all ingredients. Pour into a greased 2-quart baking dish. Bake at 350 degrees for 1 hour. Cool 10 minutes. Serves 10 to 12.

"Devilish" Ham Quiche

1   1¾-ounce package leek
     soup mix
1½ cups milk
½   cup light cream
3   eggs, slightly beaten
1½ cups grated Swiss cheese
1   teaspoon dry mustard
Dash white pepper
1   4½-ounce can deviled ham
1   baked 9-inch pie shell

Combine soup mix and milk in a 1-quart saucepan. Cook and stir until mixture boils.

Combine cream, eggs, cheese, mustard, and pepper. Stir in soup mixture.

Spread deviled ham over bottom and sides of pie shell. Pour soup mixture over ham. Bake at 325 degrees for 45 to 50 minutes. Let stand 10 minutes before cutting into wedges. Serves 6.

Onion Pie

30 saltine crackers, finely
   crumbled
¼   cup butter, melted
2½ cups thinly sliced onion
1   tablespoon butter
½   pound grated sharp
     Cheddar cheese
3   eggs, slightly beaten
1½ cups milk, scalded
Salt and pepper to taste

Combine cracker crumbs with ¼ cup butter and press into a 9-inch pie plate.

Sauté onion in 1 tablespoon butter until tender. Place in pie shell. Cover onion with grated cheese.

Combine eggs, milk, salt, and pepper and pour over cheese. Bake at 325 degrees for 30 minutes until firm. Cut into wedges. Serves 6.

Almond French Toast

8   slices bread
3   eggs
⅓   cup milk
½   teaspoon vanilla
3   ounces almond paste
2   ounces cream cheese,
      softened
4   tablespoons butter
1   tablespoon vegetable oil
Strawberry preserves

Remove crusts from bread, and process crusts in a blender until finely crumbled.

Beat together eggs, milk, and vanilla in a bowl. Set aside.

Combine almond paste and cream cheese, mixing until smooth. Spread mixture over 4 slices of bread. Top with remaining bread slices, forming 4 sandwiches. Cut each sandwich in half and dip into the egg mixture, coating well. Roll each sandwich half in the bread crumbs and dip again into the egg mixture.

Melt butter and oil in a large skillet. Cook the sandwich halves, over medium-high heat, for about 3 minutes on each side. Serve with strawberry preserves. Serves 4.

Good Morning Egg Casserole

6   hard-cooked eggs, peeled,
      halved, yolks removed
4   tablespoons mayonnaise
4   tablespoons Durkee's meat
      sauce
1   medium onion, minced
1   teaspoon paprika
4   tablespoons butter or
      margarine
4   tablespoons all-purpose
      flour
2   cups milk
1   2½-ounce package dried
      beef, shredded
½   teaspoon Worcestershire
      sauce
½   cup grated Parmesan
      cheese

Mash egg yolks and combine with mayonnaise, meat sauce, onion, and paprika. Refill egg white halves with mixture. Place in an 8 x 12-inch baking dish.

Melt butter in a saucepan, and blend in flour. Gradually add milk, cooking and stirring constantly until thick. Add shredded beef and Worcestershire sauce. Pour mixture over eggs and sprinkle with Parmesan cheese. Bake at 350 degrees for 20 to 30 minutes. Serves 6 to 8.

VEGETABLES

Cauliflower Casserole

6 tablespoons butter
4 tablespoons all-purpose
   flour
2 cups milk
Salt and pepper to taste
1 cup grated sharp Cheddar
   cheese
4 tablespoons chopped, fresh
   parsley
¼ teaspoon monosodium
   glutamate
1 tablespoon grated onion
1 large head cooked
   cauliflower, trimmed,
   reserving florets
¼ cup grated Parmesan
   cheese
Paprika

Melt butter in a small saucepan. Add flour and cook over medium heat for 1 to 2 minutes, stirring constantly. Vigorously beat in the milk with a wire whisk. Bring to a boil and cook 2 to 3 minutes more until smooth and slightly thick. Add salt and pepper.

Remove from heat and stir in cheese until melted. Mix in the parsley, monosodium glutamate, and onion.

Layer a 3-quart buttered casserole with the cauliflower and the sauce, ending with sauce. Sprinkle with Parmesan cheese and paprika. Bake at 375 degrees for 20 to 30 minutes. Serves 6 to 8.

Grilled Onions

1 Spanish onion, per person
Salt and pepper to taste
Butter

Soak whole unpeeled Spanish onions in salted water for 1 hour. Drain. Put onions on a hot grill and cook, turning frequently, until outside of skin is evenly black, about 30 minutes, or until fork pierces the skin easily. Pull back outside skin of onion and serve with salt, pepper, and butter.

Swiss Broiled Tomatoes

4 to 6 small, ripe tomatoes
Salt and pepper to taste
3 slices bread, crumbled
½ teaspoon basil
2 teaspoons butter, melted
4 slices Swiss cheese, grated

Slice tomatoes in half. Season lightly with salt and pepper. Mix remaining ingredients, and pile lightly on tomato halves. Broil until cheese begins to melt and topping is lightly browned. Serves 8 to 12.

Tomatoes Stuffed with Green Beans

2   9-ounce packages frozen
     French-style green beans
¼   cup chopped green onion
1   6-ounce jar marinated
     artichoke hearts, drained
6   medium tomatoes

Cook green beans until tender-crisp and drain. Add onion and ⅔ of the mayonnaise mixture. Add artichokes. Refrigerate overnight.

Peel tomatoes. Remove seeds and pulp and drain. Fill tomato cups with bean mixture and top with remaining mayonnaise. Serves 6.

Mayonnaise:
1   egg yolk
2½ tablespoons lemon juice
1   cup vegetable oil
⅛   teaspoon black pepper
⅛   teaspoon dill weed
⅛   teaspoon red pepper
½   teaspoon salt

Combine all ingredients.

Mushroom Stuffed Tomatoes

6   large tomatoes
1   pint mushrooms, chopped
3   tablespoons butter
2   egg yolks
½   cup sour cream
¼   cup bread crumbs
1   teaspoon salt
Dash thyme
3   tablespoons bread crumbs

Cut tops off tomatoes, scoop out flesh and turn upside down to drain. Chop flesh of tomatoes.

Sauté mushrooms in 2 tablespoons butter until tender. Beat together egg yolks and sour cream and add to mushrooms. Stir in chopped tomatoes, ¼ cup bread crumbs, salt, and thyme. Cook until mixture thickens and pour into tomato shells.

Melt 1 tablespoon butter and mix with 3 tablespoons bread crumbs. Sprinkle crumbs over filled tomatoes. Bake at 350 degrees for 25 minutes. Serves 6.

Cauliflower Soufflé

3   tablespoons butter
4   tablespoons all-purpose
     flour
1½ cups milk
6   egg yolks
½   teaspoon salt
¼   teaspoon pepper
Pinch of nutmeg
1   tablespoon chopped
     parsley
1   tablespoon chopped chives
1   garlic clove, minced
1   cup cooked cauliflower,
     trimmed and separated
     into florets
8   egg whites
Pinch of salt
⅛   teaspoon cream of tartar
¼   cup grated Parmesan
     cheese
Vegetables such as broccoli,
     peas, asparagus can be
     substituted for the
     cauliflower

Melt butter in a saucepan and stir in flour. Gradually add milk to form a thick, smooth sauce. Remove pan from heat and stir in egg yolks, one at a time. Add all seasonings and cauliflower to mixture.

Beat egg whites, salt, and cream of tartar in a large bowl until stiff. Fold in vegetable mixture. Pour into a greased 6-cup soufflé dish. Sprinkle with Parmesan cheese. Bake at 400 degrees for 25 minutes. Serves 6 to 8.

Celery Medley

4   tablespoons butter
3   cups chopped celery
1   cup chicken broth
1   3-ounce can chopped
     mushrooms, drained
1   teaspoon soy sauce
¼   teaspoon pepper
½   cup slivered almonds,
     toasted

Melt butter in a saucepan. Add celery and cook until tender-crisp. Stir in remaining ingredients. Serves 6.

Mushroom Casserole

1 cup chopped onion
½ cup butter
2 eggs, slightly beaten
¼ pound processed American cheese, cubed
½ cup half and half
2 8-ounce cans mushroom stems and pieces
¾ cup mushroom liquid
½ teaspoon salt
¼ teaspoon pepper
1 cup saltine cracker crumbs
1 or 2 tablespoons sherry

Sauté onion in butter. Combine with remaining ingredients and mix well. Pour into a 1½-quart greased casserole. Cover and bake at 350 degrees for ½ hour. Uncover and bake another ½ hour. Serves 8.

Zucchini Florentine

4 cups sliced zucchini
2 tablespoons chopped onion
1 tablespoon butter
2 eggs, beaten
1 cup mayonnaise
¾ cup grated sharp Cheddar cheese
½ cup grated Parmesan cheese
1 teaspoon seasoned salt

Microwave
Place zucchini in a 2-quart glass casserole. Cover and microwave on high for 7 minutes. Drain.

Place onion and butter in a glass measuring cup, and microwave on high for 1½ minutes.

Combine eggs, mayonnaise, cheese, and salt in a large mixing bowl. Add zucchini and return mixture to casserole dish. Microwave on high for 3 minutes. Stir, and microwave on high for 2 minutes. Serves 6.

Tropical Rice

2½ cups chicken broth
1 cup long grain white rice
1 tablespoon butter
1 cup diced celery
5 tablespoons ground, salted peanuts

Bring chicken broth to a boil in a saucepan. Stir in rice and butter. Cover and simmer over low heat for 15 minutes. Add celery and peanuts and simmer 10 more minutes or until liquid is absorbed and rice is tender. Serves 4 to 6.

Artichoke Ring

¼ pound prosciutto, sliced
2   10-ounce packages frozen
     artichoke hearts, thawed,
     drained
1 to 1½ tablespoons butter
1   medium onion, finely
     chopped
1   garlic clove, minced
4   eggs
1   cup heavy cream
½   cup freshly grated
     Parmesan cheese
Salt and pepper to taste
¼   teaspoon nutmeg

Grease a 4-cup ring mold and line with prosciutto slices. Leave 2 to 3 inches of prosciutto hanging over the edges of the mold for enclosing later.

Chop artichokes finely in a blender or food processor.

In a skillet, melt butter and sauté onion and garlic until tender. Set aside.

In a large bowl, beat eggs lightly and add cream, cheese, onion-garlic mixture, and seasonings. Stir in artichokes and pour mixture carefully into the prosciutto-lined mold. Cover top with over-hanging prosciutto. Place in a pan of hot water in the oven and bake at 350 degrees for 25 to 30 minutes or until a knife inserted in the center comes out clean. Serves 6.

Party Broccoli

2   tablespoons butter
2   tablespoons minced onion
1½ cups sour cream
2   teaspoons sugar
1   teaspoon vinegar
½   teaspoon poppy seeds
½   teaspoon paprika
½   teaspoon salt
Dash cayenne
1   bunch broccoli, cooked and
     drained, or 2 packages
     frozen broccoli
½   cup chopped cashew nuts

Melt butter in saucepan. Add onion and sauté. Remove from heat and stir in sour cream, sugar, vinegar, poppy seeds, and spices. Arrange broccoli on a platter. Top with the sauce and sprinkle with cashews. Serves 6 to 8.

Sweet and Sour Roquefort Beans

1   9-ounce package frozen
    French-style green beans
2   slices bacon
1   small onion, chopped
2   teaspoons sugar
2   teaspoons vinegar
Salt and pepper to taste
2   tablespoons crumbled
    Roquefort or bleu cheese

Cook beans until tender-crisp. Drain, reserving 2 tablespoons liquid.

Fry bacon until crisp, in a skillet. Drain. Cook onion in bacon grease until lightly browned. Add reserved bean liquid, beans, sugar, vinegar, salt, and pepper. Heat thoroughly. Spoon into a serving dish. Sprinkle with crumbled cheese. Serves 4.

Egg and Asparagus au Gratin

2½ cups cooked asparagus
    spears
4   hard-cooked eggs, sliced
1   5-ounce can water
    chestnuts, drained, sliced
1   4-ounce jar sliced pimento
2   tablespoons butter
2   tablespoons all-purpose
    flour
½   teaspoon salt
Dash pepper
1   cup milk
1   cup grated sharp Cheddar
    cheese
1   cup soft, buttered, bread
    crumbs

Arrange asparagus in a 6 x 9-inch baking dish. Place sliced egg, water chestnuts and pimento on top.

Melt butter in a saucepan. Add flour, salt, and pepper. Gradually add milk, blending thoroughly. Stir in cheese. Pour over asparagus. Sprinkle with bread crumbs. Bake at 350 degrees for about 20 minutes. Serves 4 to 6.

Eggplant au Gratin

1 to 2 pound eggplant cut into
    ½-inch slices
½   cup mayonnaise
½   cup saltine cracker crumbs
¾   cup grated Parmesan
    cheese

Coat eggplant slices with mayonnaise. Mix cracker crumbs and cheese in a bowl. Dip eggplant slices into mixture, place on a greased cookie sheet, and bake for 15 minutes. Turn slices over and bake 5 minutes more, until golden. Serves 4 to 6.

Carrots and Grapes

2   pounds tiny carrots
4   whole cloves
4   cups water
1   pound seedless green
     grapes
1   cup brown sugar
2   teaspoons cinnamon
4   ounces cornstarch
2   ounces water

Cook carrots and cloves in water until carrots are tender. Add grapes, brown sugar, and cinnamon. Dissolve cornstarch in 2 ounces of water and add to carrot mixture. Stir until thickened. Serves 8.

Eggplant Provencal

3   tablespoons vegetable oil
3   garlic cloves, minced
1   small onion, sliced
2   medium eggplants, cut into
     1-inch cubes
Salt and pepper to taste
1   6-ounce can tomato sauce
1   cup water
1   tablespoon dried oregano
Grated Parmesan cheese

Heat oil in a large skillet. Add garlic and onion and cook until tender and brown. Add eggplant and cook about 3 to 5 minutes over high heat, turning frequently, until lightly browned on all sides. Season with salt and pepper.

Cover pan and simmer 5 minutes. Add tomato sauce, water, and oregano. Cover and simmer an additional 5 minutes. Sprinkle with Parmesan cheese. Serves 4 to 6.

Spinach Noodle Casserole

2   10-ounce packages frozen
     chopped spinach
2   12-ounce packages frozen
     spinach soufflé
1   cup cottage cheese
1   cup sour cream
½   cup grated Parmesan
     cheese
1   small onion, minced
½   teaspoon Worcestershire
     sauce
1   8-ounce package egg
     noodles, cooked

Defrost the 4 packages of spinach. Drain chopped spinach and mix with the spinach soufflé. Set aside.

Mix together, in a bowl, the cottage cheese, sour cream, Parmesan cheese, onion, and Worcestershire sauce.

Combine noodles with the cheese mixture and pour into a 2½-quart casserole. Layer spinach evenly over the top. Bake at 350 degrees for 40 minutes. Serves 6 to 8.

Creamed Spinach

1 pound fresh spinach, or 2
   10½-ounce packages
   frozen chopped spinach
4 tablespoons butter
2 garlic cloves, minced
½ cup heavy cream
Salt and pepper to taste
½ teaspoon nutmeg

Cook spinach in a large saucepan for 5 to 6 minutes until tender. Drain spinach and refresh it under cold water until it is cool. Squeeze as much water as possible from the spinach, and chop finely.

Melt butter in a large skillet. Sauté garlic until it is golden. Add spinach and cook over moderately high heat, stirring until the moisture evaporates. Add 2 ounces of the cream and simmer the mixture, stirring until it is hot and the cream is well reduced. Slowly add rest of the cream, letting the additions reduce before adding more. Season with salt, pepper, and nutmeg. Serves 6.

Asparagus Soufflé

2 14-ounce cans asparagus
   spears, drained
5 slices white bread, crusts
   removed, cubed
2 cups grated cheese
½ cup butter
6 eggs
2 cups milk

Place asparagus in a 8 x 12-inch baking dish. Cover with bread cubes and cheese. Dot with butter. Beat together eggs and milk and pour over asparagus mixture. Bake at 350 degrees for 1 hour. Serves 8.

Delicious Carrots

2½ pounds carrots, julienned
1 tablespoon minced onion
½ cup mayonnaise
1 tablespoon horseradish
Salt and pepper to taste
¼ cup saltine cracker crumbs
2 tablespoons butter
1 teaspoon fresh, chopped
   parsley
1 teaspoon paprika

Cook carrots in a saucepan until tender. Reserve ¼ cup of liquid. Arrange carrots in a 2-quart baking dish. Combine carrot liquid with onion, mayonnaise, horseradish, salt, and pepper. Pour over carrots. Sprinkle cracker crumbs on top and dot with butter. Sprinkle with parsley and paprika. Bake at 375 degrees for 20 minutes. Serves 6.

Zucchini Pie

½   cup butter
4   cups unpeeled, sliced zucchini
1   cup chopped onion
½   cup chopped parsley
½   teaspoon salt
½   teaspoon pepper
¼   teaspoon garlic powder
1   teaspoon basil
½   teaspoon oregano
2   eggs
2   cups Monterey Jack cheese
1   8-ounce can crescent rolls
1   tablespoon Dijon-style mustard

Melt butter in a skillet. Mix in zucchini, onion, parsley, and seasonings and sauté until tender. Drain excess juice from vegetables. Blend together eggs and cheese. Stir into vegetable mixture.

Press crescent rolls into an ungreased pie pan. Spread formed crust with mustard. Pour zucchini mixture into crust and bake at 375 degrees for 18 to 20 minutes. Let stand 10 to 12 minutes before serving. Serves 6 to 8.

Spinach and Artichokes with Hollandaise

2   10-ounce packages frozen, chopped spinach
½   pound fresh mushrooms
6   tablespoons butter
1   tablespoon all-purpose flour
½   cup milk
½   teaspoon salt
½   teaspoon garlic powder
1   14-ounce can artichoke bottoms, drained
1   cup sour cream
1   cup mayonnaise
¼   cup lemon juice

Cook spinach according to package directions and drain well.

Reserve 16 mushroom caps. Chop remaining caps with stems and sauté in 2 tablespoons butter. Sauté 16 caps separately, in another 2 tablespoons butter.

Melt remaining 2 tablespoons butter in a saucepan. Add flour and cook until bubbly. Add milk, stirring constantly until smooth. Add seasonings, then the chopped mushrooms, and spinach. Place the artichoke bottoms in a 2-quart baking dish and cover them with the creamed spinach.

Combine the sour cream, mayonnaise, and lemon juice and heat slowly so they are thoroughly blended. Pour over spinach and place reserved mushroom caps on top. Bake at 375 degrees for 15 minutes. Serves 8.

Lima Beans with Mushrooms

1   cup butter
1   medium onion, chopped
5   stalks celery, sliced into ½-
    inch strips
1   pound fresh mushrooms,
    sliced
2   tablespoons all-purpose
    flour
½   teaspoon salt
½   teaspoon nutmeg
⅛   teaspoon pepper
½   cup heavy cream
2   10-ounce packages frozen
    lima beans, cooked

Melt butter in a saucepan. Sauté onion and celery until tender. Add mushrooms and continue cooking until tender. Stir in flour, salt, nutmeg, and pepper. Reduce heat and stir in cream. Add the cooked beans. Serves 8.

Monterey Zucchini

3   cups cooked rice
2   4-ounce cans chopped
    green chilies, drained
1   pound Monterey jack
    cheese, shredded
4   medium zucchini, thinly
    sliced and steamed until
    tender
3   large tomatoes, sliced
2   cups sour cream
2   green onions, chopped
1   teaspoon dried oregano
1½ teaspoons garlic salt

Put rice into a greased 9 x 13-inch casserole. Place green chilies on rice and cover with ½ of the cheese. Top with zucchini and tomato slices.

Combine sour cream, onions, oregano, and garlic salt and pour over tomatoes. Top with remaining cheese. Bake uncovered at 350 degrees for 30 minutes. Serves 8.

Sweet Potatoes Normandy

3   large sweet potatoes,
    cooked, peeled, and sliced
3   large apples, cored and
    sliced
½   cup brown sugar
4   tablespoons butter
½   teaspoon nutmeg
½   teaspoon cinnamon
½   cup orange juice

Place alternate layers of sweet potatoes and apples in a greased 1½-quart baking dish. Sprinkle each apple layer with divided sugar, butter, nutmeg, and cinnamon. End with apple layer on top.

Pour orange juice over mixture. Bake at 350 degrees for 30 to 40 minutes until apples are tender. Serves 6.

Potatoes Romanoff

6   cups cooked, cubed
    potatoes
2   cups cottage cheese
1   cup sour cream
1   garlic clove, minced
3   tablespoons chives
2   teaspoons salt
1   cup shredded Cheddar
    cheese

Combine all ingredients, reserving some of the cheese for topping. Pour into a 3-quart casserole. Bake at 350 degrees for 30 minutes. Top with reserved cheese, and return to the oven until melted. Serves 6.

Dilly Squash

4   cups thinly sliced yellow
    squash
¼   cup chopped onion
1   tablespoon butter or
    margarine
1   cup sour cream
1   tablespoon all-purpose
    flour
½   teaspoon seasoned salt
½   teaspoon dried dill
¼   cup cracker crumbs

Microwave

Place squash, onion, and butter in a 1½-quart casserole, and cover. Microwave on high for 7 minutes. Drain well.

Combine sour cream, flour, seasoned salt, and dill and pour over squash. Mix gently. Microwave on high 2 minutes. Stir. Sprinkle cracker crumbs over casserole. Microwave on high 1 minute. Serves 6.

Baked Bean Casserole

Beans:
1   16-ounce can baked beans
1   20-ounce can kidney
    beans, drained
2½ cups frozen baby lima
    beans, cooked, drained

Mix beans lightly together in a 2½-quart casserole. Pour sauce over beans and stir gently. Bake at 350 degrees for 45 minutes to 1 hour. Serves 10 to 12.

Sauce:
1   garlic clove, minced
1   medium onion, chopped
3   tablespoons bacon
    drippings
½   cup catchup
3   tablespoons brown sugar
1   teaspoon dry mustard
1   teaspoon salt
¼   teaspoon pepper
Liquid smoke, optional

Combine all ingredients in a bowl.

Creole Corn

2   onions, chopped
2   garlic cloves, minced
¼   cup vegetable oil
2   17-ounce cans white corn,
    undrained
1 to 2 tablespoons chili
    powder

Brown onion and garlic in oil over medium heat. Combine with corn and chili powder. Pour into a 2-quart casserole. Bake uncovered, stirring occasionally, at 325 degrees for 45 minutes. Serves 6.

Spinach Olé

2   10-ounce packages frozen,
     chopped spinach
4   tablespoons butter or
     margarine
2   tablespoons all-purpose
     flour
2   tablespoons chopped onion
1   cup milk
1   teaspoon Worcestershire
     sauce
½   teaspoon celery salt
½   teaspoon garlic salt
1   cup grated hot pepper
     cheese
½   cup grated Cheddar cheese
¼   cup bread crumbs
¼   cup grated Parmesan
     cheese
1   tablespoon butter, melted

Microwave

Cook spinach according to package directions and drain well.

Melt butter. Add flour and blend well. Add chopped onion and microwave on high for 2 minutes until onion is tender. Add milk and microwave for 4 minutes until thick. Add Worcestershire sauce, celery salt, garlic salt, hot pepper and Cheddar cheese. Microwave on high 2 minutes until cheese is melted.

Combine sauce and cooked spinach. Pour into a greased 2-quart casserole. Mix bread crumbs, Parmesan cheese, and melted butter. Sprinkle over spinach. Bake at 350 degrees for 30 minutes. Serves 4 to 6.

Brussel Sprouts and Carrots with Cashews

1½ cups water
1   chicken-flavored bouillon
     cube
1   pound fresh Brussel
     sprouts
¾   cup sliced carrots
2   tablespoons butter
½   cup dried, roasted cashew
     halves
⅛   teaspoon salt
Dash pepper

Microwave

Combine water and bouillon cube in a 2-quart dish. Microwave on high, 3 to 4 minutes until boiling. Add Brussel sprouts and carrots. Cover and microwave on high 10 minutes, stirring several times. Drain well. Add butter, cashews, and seasonings. Cover and microwave on high 1 minute. Stir to mix well. Serves 4.

Yellow Squash Sauté

3   bacon slices, cut into fourths
1   medium onion, chopped
2   tablespoons butter
2   pounds yellow squash, sliced thin
½   teaspoon salt
¼   teaspoon pepper
⅛   teaspoon garlic powder

Sauté bacon and onion in butter until tender. Add squash and seasonings. Cover and simmer over low heat 30 to 40 minutes. Serves 4.

Savory Green Bean Casserole

2   16-ounce cans green beans
4   strips bacon
2   tablespoons diced pimento
2   tablespoons red wine vinegar
½   teaspoon sugar
1   tablespoon Worcestershire sauce
¼   teaspoon dry mustard

Simmer beans, about 10 minutes, in a saucepan. Fry bacon in another pan until crisp. Add remaining ingredients to bacon. Bring to a boil, stirring constantly. Pour mixture over beans and mix well. Serves 6.

Sweet Potato Soufflé

3   cups cooked, mashed sweet potatoes
¾   cup sugar
2   eggs, beaten
2   teaspoons vanilla
½   cup butter, melted
½   cup milk
1   cup brown sugar
⅓   cup butter, melted
1   cup chopped pecans
⅓   cup all-purpose flour

Combine thoroughly the potatoes, ¾ cup sugar, eggs, vanilla, ½ cup butter, and milk. Pour mixture into a greased 10 x 10-inch casserole.

Mix brown sugar and ⅓ cup butter until crumbly. Combine pecans and flour and add to sugar mixture. Sprinkle over casserole and bake at 350 degrees for 30 minutes. Serves 8.

Spinach Tomatoes

⅓ cup butter
6 green onions, chopped
2 10-ounce packages
   chopped spinach, cooked
   and well drained
¾ cup dry stuffing mix
3 eggs, beaten
½ teaspoon thyme
1 teaspoon pepper
Salt to taste
6 to 10 tomatoes

Melt butter in a large saucepan. Cook onions until tender. Stir in remaining ingredients, except tomatoes, mixing well.

Cut tomatoes into thick slices and place on cookie sheets. Mound spinach mixture on slices. Bake at 350 degrees for 15 to 20 minutes. Serves 8 to 10.

Cheese and Mushroom Bake

¼ cup chopped onion
½ cup chopped celery
3 tablespoons butter
¼ pound fresh mushrooms
4 cups day-old bread, cubed
2 cups grated sharp Cheddar
   cheese
2 eggs
2 cups milk
2 teaspoons dry mustard
1 teaspoon salt
½ teaspoon pepper

Sauté onion and celery in butter. Add mushrooms and cook until tender. In a greased 2-quart casserole, layer with half of the bread cubes, vegetable mixture, and the cheese. Repeat layers.

Beat together eggs, milk, and seasonings. Pour evenly over casserole ingredients. Bake at 325 degrees for 45 minutes. Serves 6 to 8.

Candied Tomatoes

2   tablespoons butter
¼   cup chopped onion
2   16-ounce cans tomatoes
8   tablespoons brown sugar
¾   teaspoon salt
1   cup buttered bread crumbs

Melt butter in a large saucepan and sauté onion. Add tomatoes and 6 tablespoons of the brown sugar. Cook slowly until juice has been absorbed.

Place tomatoes in a 6 x 10-inch glass baking dish. Sprinkle with salt, remaining 2 tablespoons brown sugar, and bread crumbs. Bake at 350 degrees until browned. Serves 6.

Asparagus Oriental

4   tablespoons butter
1½ pounds fresh asparagus,
    cut diagonally into bite
    size pieces
1   teaspoon salt
1   teaspoon monosodium
    glutamate
½   teaspoon pepper

Melt butter over high heat, in a large heavy skillet or wok, until foam subsides. Add asparagus and seasonings. Cook, stirring constantly over high heat for 4 to 5 minutes, or until tender but still crunchy. Serves 6.

Strawberry Mousse

1   3-ounce package
    strawberry-flavored
    gelatin
1   cup boiling water
1   envelope unflavored
    gelatin
1   tablespoon cold water
1   16-ounce package frozen
    strawberries, thawed
2   tablespoons sugar
1½ cups vanilla ice cream
1   cup heavy cream
Fresh or frozen strawberries

Dissolve strawberry gelatin in boiling water. Dissolve unflavored gelatin in 1 tablespoon cold water and add to strawberry gelatin. Puree frozen strawberries in a blender. Add gelatin mixture and sugar to the frozen strawberries and blend again.

Add ice cream and cream, blending well. Pour mixture into a wet 6-cup ring mold. Freeze. To serve, unmold and let defrost 15 minutes. Fill the center of the gelatin ring with fresh or frozen strawberries. Serves 8.

Tropical Fruit Fluff

1   cup sour cream
½   cup flaked coconut
2   tablespoons chopped
    walnuts
2   tablespoons chopped
    apricot preserves
1   tablespoon milk
1   walnut half
6 to 8 cups fresh grapes,
    melon balls, pineapple,
    sliced bananas,
    strawberries, or a
    combination

Combine sour cream, ¼ cup coconut, chopped walnuts, and preserves in a small bowl, mixing well. Stir in milk.

Pour into a serving dish and garnish with the walnut half and remaining ¼ cup coconut. Serve separately as a dip or spoon over fresh fruit. Serves 6 to 8.

Tangerine Sherbet

2   cups fresh tangerine juice
1   cup sugar
1   cup milk

Combine tangerine juice and sugar and stir until sugar is dissolved. Add milk. Chill. Freeze in ice cream freezer. Serves 6.

Crème Brulle

Sauce:
2   cups heavy cream
2   tablespoons sugar
¾   cup light brown sugar
5   egg yolks, well beaten
2   teaspoons vanilla, or to
    taste

Heat cream in top of a double boiler. Add sugar, brown sugar, and egg yolks, stirring constantly to avoid curdling. Cook over medium heat, reducing to low as necessary, until mixture coats a spoon. Cover and refrigerate overnight. Just before serving, add vanilla.

8   canned peach halves
8   teaspoons butter
8   teaspoon brown sugar
8   teaspoons dark rum

Place peach halves, cut side up in a 9 x 13-inch shallow baking dish. Into each peach place 1 teaspoon butter, 1 teaspoon sugar, and 1 teaspoon rum. Let set several hours, basting occasionally with the rum. Broil 4 to 5 minutes until brown and bubbly.

Serve very cold sauce over very hot peaches. Serves 4.

Chocolate Peanut Dessert

½   cup butter or margarine,
    softened
1   cup all-purpose flour
1   cup finely chopped dry-
    roasted peanuts
1   8-ounce package cream
    cheese
⅓   cup peanut butter
1   cup confectioners' sugar
1   12-ounce container frozen
    non-dairy whipped
    topping, thawed
1   4⅛-ounce package instant
    chocolate pudding
1   4⅛-ounce package instant
    vanilla pudding
2¾ cups milk

Cut butter into flour until crumbly. Stir in ⅔ cup chopped peanuts. Press mixture into a 9 x 13-inch pan. Bake at 350 degrees for 20 minutes. Cool.

Combine cream cheese, peanut butter, and confectioners' sugar, beating until fluffy. Stir in 1 cup whipped topping and spread mixture over prepared crust. Chill.

Combine vanilla and chocolate pudding with milk. Beat 2 minutes. Spread pudding over cream cheese layer. Spread remaining whipped topping over pudding. Sprinkle with remaining ⅓ cup chopped peanuts. Refrigerate overnight. Serves 15.

Orange Charlotte

1   tablespoon unflavored
     gelatin
¼   cup cold water
½   cup boiling water
1   cup orange juice
Juice of ½ lemon
1   cup sugar
2   cups heavy cream, whipped
1   angel food loaf cake or ½
     of a 10-inch tube cake,
     broken into pieces
Almond slivers
Orange or fruit slices

Soften gelatin in ½ cup cold water. Add ½ cup boiling water, orange juice, lemon juice, and sugar. Cool. When partly gelled, add whipped cream and cake pieces. Pour into a serving dish and refrigerate until set. Garnish with slivered almonds and orange or fruit slices. Serves 8 to 10.

Grand Marnier Soufflé

9   eggs, separated
⅔   cup sugar
1   6-ounce can frozen orange
     juice concentrate, thawed
Rind of 1 orange, coarsely
     grated
Juice of 1 lemon
1   ounce Grand Marnier

Warm egg yolks in top of a double boiler, and then beat until light and fluffy. Add sugar and cook about 5 minutes until mixture is slightly thickened. Remove from heat. Stir in orange juice concentrate. Add grated orange rind, lemon juice and Grand Marnier.

Beat egg whites until stiff, but not dry. Fold in orange mixture. Pour into a butter and sugar coated 2-quart soufflé dish. Bake at 350 degrees for 18 to 20 minutes. Soufflé should be soft in the center. Serve immediately. Serves 8 to 10.

Peach Ice Cream

1   pint peeled, mashed,
     peaches
1¼ cups sugar
1   teaspoon lemon juice
2   cups milk
4   cups heavy cream

Combine all ingredients in a blender or food processor. Freeze in ice cream freezer. Serves 8.

Margarita Soufflé

10 **eggs, separated**
1   **cup sugar**
1   **cup lime juice**
Grated rind of 4 limes
1   **teaspoon salt**
2   **envelopes unflavored gelatin**
½   **cup tequila**
½   **cup triple sec**
2   **cups heavy cream, whipped**

Beat egg yolks with an electric mixer on high speed until light and fluffy. Gradually add sugar and beat until smooth and light yellow. Mix in lime juice, rind, and salt. Pour mixture into top of a double boiler and cook, over boiling water, until thickened, about 10 to 15 minutes, stirring constantly.

Sprinkle gelatin over tequila and triple sec in a small saucepan. Cook over low heat until gelatin dissolves, stirring constantly. Gradually pour into hot custard mixture, and stir until well combined. Chill.

Beat egg whites until stiff peaks form; fold into custard. Fold in whipped cream.

Butter a 2-quart soufflé dish and make a paper collar around outside of dish and tape in place. Pour mixture into soufflé dish. Refrigerate overnight. Serves 12.

Chocolate Cheese Cake

Crust:
½   **cup butter, melted**
2   **cups graham cracker crumbs**
6   **tablespoons sugar**

Brush sides and bottom of a 9-inch springform pan with some of the melted butter. Combine remaining butter, graham cracker crumbs, and sugar. Press mixture into sides and bottom of pan.

Filling:
8   **1-ounce squares semi-sweet chocolate, melted**
3   **8-ounce packages cream cheese, softened**
1   **cup sugar**
2   **eggs**
2   **teaspoons cocoa**
1   **teaspoon vanilla**
1½ **cups sour cream**

Combine all ingredients except sour cream; mix well and stir in sour cream. Spoon into prepared crust. Bake at 350 degrees for 45 minutes. Cool at room temperature for 1 hour.

Cake will be soft in the middle and will have shrunk from sides of pan after baking, but will firm up as it cools. Refrigerate overnight. Serves 16.

Pears Praised

2 16-ounce cans pear halves, drained, reserving ⅔ cup juice
2 tablespoons butter
3 tablespoons dark brown sugar
1 cup dry white wine
1 cup heavy cream
6 tablespoons confectioners' sugar
⅔ cup dry sherry
Nutmeg

Arrange pear halves, cut-side up, in a buttered 9 x 13-inch baking dish. Dot pears with butter and sprinkle with brown sugar.

Combine reserved pear juice with wine and pour over pears. Bake at 400 degrees for 25 to 30 minutes.

Whip cream with confectioners' sugar until stiff. Fold in sherry. Spoon into a serving dish and sprinkle with nutmeg. Serve with warm pears. Serves 6 to 8.

Pumpkin Torte

1½ cups graham cracker crumbs
⅓ cup sugar
½ cup butter, melted
2 eggs
1 8-ounce package cream cheese
½ cup sugar
1¼ cups canned pumpkin
½ cup milk
3 eggs, separated
½ cup sugar
½ teaspoon salt
1 teaspoon cinnamon
1 teaspoon allspice
2 envelopes unflavored gelatin
¾ cup cold water
¼ cup confectioners' sugar
1 cup heavy cream
1 teaspoon vanilla
2 tablespoons sugar

Combine crumbs, ⅓ cup sugar, and butter. Press mixture into bottom and sides of a 9 x 13-inch pan. Beat 2 eggs, cream cheese, and ½ cup sugar together. Pour over crust. Bake at 325 degrees for 20 minutes. Cool.

Mix pumpkin, milk, 3 egg yolks, ½ cup sugar, salt, cinnamon, and allspice together in a saucepan. Cook until mixture thickens.

Dissolve gelatin in cold water and add to cooked pumpkin mixture. Cool. Beat egg whites. Add confectioners' sugar and beat until stiff peaks form. Fold into pumpkin mixture. Pour over cooled cheese layer and refrigerate until set. Whip cream with vanilla and 2 tablespoons sugar. Cover pumpkin torte with cream and refrigerate overnight. Serves 16.

Hot Fudge Pudding

1   cup all-purpose flour
2   teaspoons baking powder
¾   cup sugar
2   tablespoons cocoa
½   cup milk
2   tablespoons butter, melted
1   cup nuts, optional
1   cup brown sugar
¼   cup cocoa
2   cups hot water
Ice cream

Combine flour, baking powder, ¾ cup sugar, and 2 tablespoons cocoa. Blend in milk and butter. Spread mixture in a greased 8 x 8-inch pan. Top with nuts, if desired.

Sprinkle with brown sugar and ¼ cup cocoa. Pour hot water over top and immediately place in oven. Bake at 350 degrees for 45 minutes. Serve hot or cold with ice cream. Serves 6.

Caramel Flan

1¼ cups sugar, divided
2   tablespoons brandy
2   cups milk
2   cups light cream
6   eggs
½   teaspoon salt
2   teaspoons vanilla
⅓   cup brandy
Boiling water
1   tablespoon brandy

Combine ¾ cup sugar and 1 tablespoon brandy in a heavy saucepan. Cook and blend over medium heat until sugar melts and forms a light brown syrup. Immediately pour syrup into a heated, 9-inch round, shallow, glass baking dish. Hold dish with pot holders and quickly rotate dish to cover bottom and sides completely with syrup. Set aside.

Combine milk and cream in a medium saucepan. Heat just until bubbles form around edge of pan.

Slightly beat eggs in a large bowl. Add ½ cup sugar, salt, and vanilla. Gradually stir in hot milk mixture. Add ⅓ cup brandy. Pour into prepared dish. Place dish in a shallow pan and pour boiling water ½-inch deep around dish. Bake at 325 degrees for 35 to 40 minutes or until a knife inserted in center comes out clean. Cool. Refrigerate overnight.

To serve, run a small spatula around edge of dish to loosen. Invert flan on a serving plate, shaking gently to release. The caramel acts as a sauce. Serves 8 to 10.

Bananas Carrara

¼ cup butter
½ cup brown sugar
½ teaspoon allspice
4 bananas, peeled, split
  lengthwise in halves
2 ounces Grand Marnier
Juice of 1 orange
½ cup canned, grated coconut
  in extra heavy syrup
1 ounce brandy
2 tablespoons grated orange
  rind

Melt and clarify butter in a crepe pan or other shallow pan. Stir in sugar and allspice. Place bananas in butter mixture and simmer until brown.

Add Grand Marnier and orange juice and simmer 2 to 3 minutes. Spread coconut and syrup over bananas. Top with brandy and orange rind. Ignite and serve immediately. Serves 4.

Key Lime Italian Ice

1 key lime
1 cup sugar
4 cups water
Dash salt
½ cup key lime juice

Remove zest, the colored part of the rind, from 1 key lime, and cut into small pieces. Place zest and sugar in a blender or food processor, and blend until zest is finely chopped. Pour mixture into a 3-quart saucepan. Add water and salt and heat until sugar dissolves. Cool.

Add enough water to lime juice to make ⅔ cup liquid. Stir into cooled sugar mixture. Pour into divided ice cube trays and freeze.

Place frozen cubes in blender or processor and process until cubes become a velvety slush. Scoop into individual goblets or store, covered, in the freezer. Makes about 4½ cups.

Oreo Ice Cream

1 quart vanilla ice cream,
  softened
20 to 25 Oreo cookies,
  crumbled
1 6-ounce can frozen
  lemonade concentrated,
  thawed

Combine ice cream, cookie crumbs, and lemonade, mixing well. Pour into a 2-quart container. Cover and freeze overnight. Serves 6 to 8.

Pavlova

4	**egg whites**
1	**cup sugar**
1	**teaspoon vinegar**
1	**teaspoon vanilla**
1	**rounded tablespoon cornstarch**
2	**cups heavy cream, whipped**
3	**cups fresh fruit: sliced strawberries, sliced peaches, blueberries, or a combination**

Beat egg whites in a large bowl until foamy. Gradually add sugar, continuing to beat at high speed until whites stand in peaks. Fold in vinegar, vanilla, and cornstarch.

Cut an 8-inch circle of waxed paper. Butter both sides of paper and place on a cookie sheet. Spread the egg white mixture evenly over the paper. Bake at 250 degrees for 1¼ hours. Cool.

Remove paper and place meringue on a serving platter. Cover completely with whipped cream and top with fresh fruit. Serves 6 to 8.

Almond Cream Soufflé

3	**tablespoons butter**
3	**tablespoons all-purpose flour**
1	**cup light cream**
½	**cup sugar**
4	**egg yolks**
¾	**cup ground almonds**
½	**teaspoon almond extract**
6	**egg whites**
Pinch of salt	
⅛	**teaspoon cream of tartar**
⅓	**cup sliced or slivered almonds, toasted**

Butter a 4-cup soufflé dish and dust with confectioners' sugar. Preheat oven to 400 degrees.

Melt butter in a 1½-quart saucepan. Add flour and cook over medium heat 1 to 2 minutes, stirring constantly. Add cream, beating vigorously with a wire whisk, until combined. Continue stirring until mixture boils and becomes thick and smooth. Remove from heat. Add sugar. Beat in egg yolks, one at a time. Add almonds and almond extract.

Beat egg whites in a large bowl with salt and cream of tartar until stiff. Fold in almond mixture. Pour into prepared dish. Place in oven and reduce temperature to 375 degrees. Bake 20 minutes. Garnish with toasted almonds. Serves 6.

French Chocolate Tortoni

½   cup butter
½   cup sugar
2   1-ounce squares
    unsweetened chocolate,
    melted, cooled
2   eggs
1   4½-ounce container frozen,
    whipped topping, thawed
Chopped nuts

Cream butter. Blend in sugar, beating until light and fluffy. Add chocolate. Add eggs, one at a time, beating at high speed for 5 minutes after each addition. Fold in whipped topping. Spoon into a serving dish or individual cups. Sprinkle with nuts. Freeze 4 or more hours. Serves 8.

Grapefruit Meringue

4   grapefruit, peeled,
    sectioned
3   ounces dark rum
Brown sugar to taste
8   egg whites
¼   teaspoon salt
½   cup sugar

Arrange grapefruit sections in bottom of a greased 2½-quart soufflé dish. Sprinkle with rum and brown sugar. Bake at 350 degrees for 15 minutes.

Beat egg whites and salt in a large bowl until frothy. Beat in sugar, a little at a time, until meringue is stiff and glossy. Spread meringue over the baked grapefruit, swirling attractively. Bake at 450 degrees for a few minutes until browned, watching carefully. Serves 8.

Apple Torte

1   egg, slightly beaten
¾   cup sugar
¾   cup peeled, chopped apples
½   cup all-purpose flour
¼   teaspoon almond extract
1   teaspoon baking powder
Pinch of salt
Whipped cream or ice cream

Combine egg, sugar, and apples. Stir in flour, almond extract, baking powder, and salt. Pour into a well greased 9-inch pie pan. Bake at 350 degrees for 25 minutes. Top with whipped cream or ice cream. Serves 4 to 5.

Peach Delight

¾   cup butter
3   egg yolks
1½ cups confectioners' sugar
1   12-ounce box vanilla
    wafers, crushed
2   cups heavy cream, whipped
1   29-ounce can sliced
    peaches, drained
1   cup chopped nuts

Melt butter in a saucepan. Add egg yolks and confectioners' sugar. Cook over low heat, stirring until thickened.

Place ¾ of the vanilla wafer crumbs in a 9 x 12-inch shallow pan. Add the cooked egg mixture and mix with the crumbs. Layer half of the whipped cream over the crumb mixture. Top with a layer of sliced peaces. Sprinkle with nuts. Cover nuts with remaining whipped cream. Top with remaining vanilla wafer crumbs. Refrigerate overnight. Serves 10.

Brandy Alexander Soufflé

2   envelopes unflavored
    gelatin
2   cups cold water
1   cup sugar
4   eggs, separated
1   8-ounce package cream
    cheese, softened
3   tablespoons crème de
    cacao
3   tablespoons brandy
1   cup heavy cream, whipped
Grated chocolate

Soften gelatin in 1 cup water. Stir over low heat until dissolved. Add remaining 1 cup water and remove from heat.

Blend in ¾ cup sugar. Beat egg yolks and add to mixture. Cook 2 to 3 minutes, or until slightly thickened. Gradually add cream cheese, mixing well until blended. Stir in crème de cacao and brandy. Chill until slightly thickened.

Beat egg whites until soft peaks form. Add remaining ¼ cup sugar, continuing to beat. Fold egg whites and whipped cream into cream cheese mixture. Pour into an 8-inch spring-form pan. Refrigerate overnight. Sprinkle with grated chocolate. Serves 8.

Chocolate Mousse

1   6-ounce package semi-
    sweet chocolate morsels
1   egg
2   eggs, separated
1   teaspoon rum
Pinch of salt
1   cup heavy cream, whipped
1   teaspoon vanilla

Melt chocolate morsels in top of a double boiler. Remove from heat and beat in 1 egg. Add egg yolks, one at a time. Add rum.

Beat egg whites with pinch of salt until stiff peaks form. Add vanilla to whipped cream. Fold egg whites, and then whipped cream, into chocolate mixture. Pour into parfait glasses and refrigerate. Serves 4.

Chocolate Charlotte Russe

4   1-ounce squares
    unsweetened chocolate
¾   cup sugar
⅓   cup milk
6   eggs, separated
1½ cups unsalted butter
1½ cups confectioners' sugar
⅛   teaspoon salt
1½ teaspoons vanilla
3   3-ounce packages
    ladyfingers, split
1   cup heavy cream, whipped
Shaved, unsweetened
    chocolate

Melt chocolate squares in top of a double boiler. Mix sugar, milk and egg yolks together. Add to melted chocolate and cook until thick, stirring constantly. Cool.

Cream butter. Add ¾ cup confectioners' sugar, mixing thoroughly. Add chocolate mixture and beat well.

Beat egg whites with salt until stiff. Gradually beat in remaining ¾ cup confectioners' sugar. Fold into chocolate mixture. Add vanilla.

Line bottom and sides of a 9-inch spring-form pan with 2 packages of split ladyfingers. Pour in ½ of the chocolate mixture. Place the remaining split ladyfingers in a single layer on the chocolate mixture. Pour on remaining chocolate. Refrigerate overnight. Serve garnished with whipped cream and shaved chocolate. Serves 8.

Frozen Grand Marnier Soufflé with Strawberry Sauce

12 almond macaroons,
  crumbled
½ gallon vanilla ice cream,
  softened
5 tablespoons Grand Marnier
2 cups heavy cream, whipped
½ cup chopped, toasted
  almonds
Confectioners' sugar

Stir macaroons into softened ice cream and add Grand Marnier. Fold whipped cream into ice cream mixture. Spoon into a 10-inch tube pan. Sprinkle with almonds and confectioners' sugar.

Cover with foil and freeze overnight. Unmold and return to freezer until serving time.

Strawberry Sauce:
3 10-ounce packages frozen,
  sliced strawberries
¼ cup sugar
5 tablespoons Grand Marnier

Simmer strawberries and sugar together in a saucepan. Remove from heat and stir in Grand Marnier. Serve frozen soufflé topped with warm strawberry sauce. Serves 12.

Frozen Cheese Cake

4 3-ounce packages cream
  cheese, softened
1 cup sugar
2 eggs, separated
1 cup heavy cream, whipped
1 prepared 9-inch graham
  cracker crust

Combine cream cheese, sugar, and egg yolks. Fold in whipped cream.

Beat egg whites and fold into egg yolk mixture. Pour into pie crust. Freeze 6 hours or overnight. Thaw 20 minutes before serving. Serves 8.

Frozen Fruit Torte

1 8-ounce package cream cheese, softened
¾ cup sugar
1 12-ounce container non-dairy whipped topping, thawed
1 8-ounce can pineapple chunks, drained
1 20-ounce can crushed pineapple
1 10-ounce package frozen strawberries with juice, thawed
½ cup chopped nuts
1 11-ounce package coconut bar cookies, crushed
½ cup butter or margarine, melted

Combine cream cheese, sugar and whipped topping until creamy. Add fruits and nuts.

Mix cookie crumbs with butter and press into bottom and sides of a 9 x 13-inch pan, reserving about ½ cup to cover top of dessert. Pour fruit and cheese mixture into pan; cover with remaining crumbs. Freeze overnight. Remove from freezer 15 minutes before serving and cut into squares. Serves 15.

Sauce Licor De Café

1 cup sugar
1 cup water
1 teaspoon instant coffee powder
⅛ teaspoon cinnamon
⅛ teaspoon ground cloves
⅛ teaspoon ground nutmeg
¼ cup coffee flavored liqueur
Coffee ice cream
Slivered toasted almonds

Combine sugar with water in a saucepan. Add instant coffee, cinnamon, cloves, and nutmeg, stirring over low heat until dissolved. Bring to a boil and boil slowly for 5 minutes. Skim off any residue that rises to the surface. Cool.

Stir in coffee flavored liqueur. Serve over coffee ice cream, garnished with toasted almonds. Sauce will keep indefinitely in refrigerator. Makes 13 ounces of sauce.

Date Crumble

2 eggs
1 cup sugar
1 tablespoon all-purpose flour
2 teaspoons baking powder
1 cup chopped nuts
1 cup chopped dates
2 cups heavy cream, whipped

Beat eggs and gradually add sugar. Combine flour, baking powder, nuts, and dates in a separate bowl. Add to egg and sugar mixture, combining well.

Spread mixture into 2 9-inch pie pans. Bake at 300 degrees for 45 minutes. Cool. Crumble into small pieces. Fold whipped cream into crumbs. Spoon into a large serving bowl or into individual compotes. Serves 6 to 8.

Palm Beach Gold

1 cup heavy cream
½ cup confectioners' sugar
1 cup miniature marshmallows
1 cup shredded pineapple
1½ cups papaya balls
1 cup orange segments

Whip cream, gradually adding sugar, until stiff peaks form. Fold in marshmallows and fruit. Pour into a serving dish or individual glass dishes. Chill well. Serves 4.

Lychee Sherbet

20 to 24 lychees, peeled, seeds removed
1 envelope unflavored gelatin
¼ cup cold water
⅔ cup milk
⅓ to ½ cup sugar
1 cup light cream
1 teaspoon lemon juice

Squeeze lychees through 2 thicknesses of cheesecloth to obtain 1 cup juice.

Sprinkle gelatin over cold water and let stand 5 minutes. Scald ⅓ cup of the milk, add soaked gelatin, and stir until thoroughly dissolved. Add sugar, mixing well. Cool. Add remaining ⅓ cup milk and the cream. Stir in lychee juice and lemon juice. Freeze in an ice cream freezer. Serves 6.

Marbled Chocolate Rum Pie

1 envelope unflavored
gelatin
¼ cup sugar
¼ teaspoon salt
2 eggs, separated
1 cup milk
¼ cup dark rum
1 teaspoon rum extract
1 12-ounce package semi-
sweet chocolate morsels
¾ cup sugar
1 cup heavy cream
1 teaspoon vanilla
1 baked 10-inch pie shell

Mix gelatin, ¼ cup sugar, and salt in top of a double boiler. Beat in egg yolks, milk, rum, and rum extract. Cook over boiling water, stirring constantly until slightly thickened. Stir in chocolate morsels until melted. Chill until thickened.

In separate bowl, beat egg whites until foamy. Add ½ cup sugar and beat until stiff. Fold into cooled chocolate mixture.

Whip cream with remaining ¼ cup sugar and the vanilla. Pour into pie shell alternating with the chocolate mixture, swirling for marble-like effect. Chill until firm. Makes 1 pie.

Mocha Date Pie

¾ cup strong, hot coffee
32 regular-size marshmallows,
cut-up
1 cup finely chopped dates
⅛ teaspoon salt
1 teaspoon vanilla
¾ cup heavy cream, whipped
1 baked 9-inch, deep dish pie
shell

Pour coffee into a large saucepan. Add marshmallows and dates and stir over low heat until marshmallows melt. Add salt and vanilla. Cool. Add cream to coffee mixture. Pour into pie shell. Refrigerate or freeze and serve frozen. Makes 1 pie.

Lemon Curd Pie

3 eggs
1 egg yolk
1 cup sugar
Grated rind of 2 lemons
Juice of 2 lemons
½ cup butter
1 baked 9-inch pie shell
Whipped cream for garnish

Place eggs, egg yolk, and sugar in top of a double boiler. Stir in grated lemon rind, lemon juice, and butter. Cook, stirring constantly, until mixture thickens, 15 to 20 minutes. Cool. Spoon into pie shell. Chill. Garnish with whipped cream. Makes 1 pie.

Sweet Potato Pie

2   cups sugar
1   cup butter
4   eggs
2   cups cooked, mashed sweet
    potatoes
4   ounces whisky
Juice and grated rind of 1
    lemon
2   unbaked 9-inch pie shells
Confectioners' sugar

Cream sugar and butter. Add eggs and potatoes. Add whisky, lemon rind and juice. Pour mixture into pie shells. Bake at 350 degrees for 50 to 60 minutes. Cool. Sprinkle with confectioners' sugar. Makes 2 pies.

Fudge Sundae Pie

1   6-ounce package chocolate
    morsels
1   cup evaporated milk
1½ cups miniature
    marshmallows
½   teaspoon salt
1   quart vanilla ice cream
1   prepared 9-inch graham
    cracker crust
1   cup chopped pecans

Microwave
Place morsels, milk, marshmallows, and salt in a glass bowl and microwave on high for 4 minutes, stirring at 1 minute intervals, until mixture is melted. Cool completely.

Spoon ½ of the ice cream into the pie crust. Cover ice cream with ½ of the chocolate sauce. Top with remaining ice cream followed by fudge sauce. Sprinkle with nuts and freeze until firm. Makes 1 pie.

Frozen Raspberry Pie

1   10-ounce package frozen
    raspberries, thawed
1   cup sugar
2   egg whites
¼   teaspoon almond extract
1   tablespoon lemon juice
Dash salt
1   cup heavy cream, whipped
2   prepared 9-inch graham
    cracker crusts

Combine the first 6 ingredients in a bowl and whip for 15 minutes. Fold in cream. Pour into pie crusts and freeze. Serve frozen. Makes 2 pies.

Peachy Ice Cream Pie

Crust:

1⅓ cups graham cracker
  crumbs
¼   cup butter, softened
¼   cup sugar

  Combine ingredients until crumbly. Press firmly onto sides and bottom of an ungreased 9-inch pie pan. Bake at 375 degrees for 8 minutes. Cool.

Filling:

1   quart peach ice cream
⅓   cup amaretto

  Combine ice cream and amaretto. Pour mixture into crust. Freeze until hard.

Meringue:

3   egg whites
½   teaspoon vanilla
¼   teaspoon cream of tartar
6   tablespoons sugar

  Beat egg whites, vanilla, and cream of tartar until soft peaks form. Gradually add sugar, beating until stiff and glossy. Cover ice cream with meringue, making sure to spread to edges. Place pie on a wooden board and bake at 475 degrees for 2 to 3 minutes or until lightly browned. Serve immediately. Makes 1 pie.

Fudge Pie

2   eggs
1   cup sugar
¼   cup all-purpose flour
⅛   teaspoon salt
2   1-ounce squares
  unsweetened chocolate
½   cup butter
1   unbaked 9-inch pie shell

  Beat eggs and sugar together. Add flour and salt and beat well.
  In a saucepan, melt chocolate and butter. Add to flour mixture and beat well. Pour into pie shell and bake at 350 degrees for 25 minutes. Makes 1 pie.

Heavenly Chocolate Pie

Crust:

1½ cups chocolate cookie
  crumbs
¼ cup butter, softened
1 tablespoon sugar

Combine ingredients and press mixture firmly into an ungreased 9-inch pie pan. Chill.

Filling:

⅓ cup amaretto
1 quart chocolate-almond ice
  cream, softened

Stir amaretto into ice cream. Pour mixture into chilled pie shell. Freeze until hard.

Topping:

1 cup heavy cream
2 tablespoons amaretto
Chocolate sprinkles

Combine cream and amaretto and beat until stiff. Mound whipped cream around outer edges of pie. Garnish with chocolate sprinkles. Freeze. Makes 1 pie.

Brandy Alexander Pie

1 envelope unflavored
  gelatin
½ cup cold water
⅛ teaspoon salt
3 eggs, separated
⅔ cup sugar
½ cup brandy
⅓ cup crème de cocoa
2 cups heavy cream, whipped
1 prepared 9-inch graham
  cracker crust
Grated dark chocolate,
  optional

Sprinkle gelatin over cold water in a saucepan. Add salt, egg yolks, and ⅓ cup sugar. Stir to blend, heating until gelatin dissolves and mixture thickens. Remove from heat and stir in brandy and crème de cocoa. Chill until mixture slightly mounds, usually about 30 minutes.

In a separate bowl, beat egg whites until stiff. Gradually add remaining ⅓ cup sugar. Add to gelatin mixture. Add half of whipped cream and mix well. Pour into crust. Chill overnight in refrigerator. Garnish with the remaining whipped cream and grated dark chocolate. Makes 1 pie.

Florida Strawberry Cream Pie

Crust:
2½ cups flaked coconut
⅓ cup butter, melted

Combine coconut and butter. Press into a 9-inch pie plate. Bake at 300 degrees for 30 to 35 minutes or until golden brown. Cool.

Filling:
2 pints fresh strawberries, stems removed
¾ cup sugar
1 envelope unflavored gelatin
½ cup water
2 teaspoons lemon juice
1 cup heavy cream, whipped

Thinly slice 1½ pints strawberries. Combine with sugar and set aside until sugar dissolves.

Soften gelatin in water. Stir over low heat until gelatin dissolves. Combine gelatin, strawberry-sugar mixture, and lemon juice. Fold in whipped cream. Chill about 2 hours or until mixture mounds when dropped from a spoon. Pour filling into crust. Chill 4 hours or until set. Garnish with remaining strawberries. Makes 1 pie.

Peaches 'n Cream Pie

¾ cup all-purpose flour
1 teaspoon baking powder
½ teaspoon salt
1 3¼-ounce package vanilla pudding mix (not instant)
3 tablespoons butter, softened
1 egg
½ cup milk
1 15-ounce can sliced freestone peaches, well drained, reserving 3 tablespoons syrup
½ cup sugar
1 8-ounce package cream cheese
1 tablespoon sugar
¼ teaspoon cinnamon

Combine flour, baking powder, salt, pudding mix, butter, egg, and milk and mix 2 minutes. Pour into a 9-inch pie pan. Place peaches on top.

Combine peach syrup, sugar, and cream cheese and beat 2 minutes. Spoon this mixture over the peaches to within 1-inch of the edge of the batter.

Combine, in another bowl, sugar and cinnamon and sprinkle over the cream cheese. Bake at 350 degrees for 30 to 35 minutes until crust is golden brown. Filling will appear soft. Can be served warm or cold. Makes 1 pie.

Quickie Orange Pie

1   12-ounce container non-
    dairy whipped topping
1   14-ounce can sweetened
    condensed milk
½   cup lemon juice
2   11-ounce cans mandarin
    oranges, drained, cut into
    pieces
2   prepared 9-inch graham
    cracker crusts

Mix together the whipped topping, sweetened condensed milk, and lemon juice in a
large bowl. Stir in oranges. Pour into pie
shells. Refrigerate. Makes 2 pies.

Pecan Cream Cheese Pie

1   8-ounce package cream
    cheese
4   eggs
⅓   cup plus ¼ cup sugar
2   teaspoons vanilla
1   unbaked 10-inch pie shell
1¼ cups coarsely chopped
    pecans
1   cup light corn syrup
¼   teaspoon salt

Mix cream cheese, 1 egg, ⅓ cup sugar, and 1
teaspoon vanilla in a bowl. Pour into pie shell
and sprinkle with pecans.
Beat the remaining 3 eggs in another bowl,
until frothy. Add corn syrup, ¼ cup sugar, ¼
teaspoon salt, and 1 teaspoon vanilla. Mix
until blended. Gently pour mixture over
pecans. Bake at 375 degrees for 40 minutes or
until an inserted knife comes out clean. Cool.
Makes 1 pie.

Banberry Pie

2   10-ounce packages frozen
    strawberries, thawed,
    drained, reserving syrup
1   tablespoon lemon juice
5   tablespoons sugar
2   teaspoons cornstarch
¼   teaspoon salt
1   baked 9-inch pie shell
½   cup chopped pecans
2   bananas, sliced
1   cup heavy cream, whipped

Combine drained strawberry syrup and
lemon juice in a saucepan. Add sugar, cornstarch, and salt. Cook over medium heat until
very thick. Cool. Fold in strawberries.
Line pie shell with pecans. Place banana
slices on top of pecans. Pour strawberry mixture over bananas. Chill. Top with whipped
cream. Makes 1 pie.

Buttermilk Coconut Pie

3   eggs, beaten
1   tablespoon all-purpose
    flour
1¼ cups sugar
1   teaspoon vanilla
1½ cups coconut
½   cup buttermilk
6   tablespoons butter, melted
1   unbaked 9-inch pie shell
Nutmeg

Combine flour and sugar and add to eggs in a large bowl, mixing thoroughly. Add vanilla, coconut, buttermilk, and butter. Pour mixture into pie shell and sprinkle with nutmeg. Bake at 350 degrees for 1 hour. Cover pie with foil if it starts to brown. Makes 1 pie.

Calamondin Pie

1   14-ounce can sweetened
    condensed milk
⅓   cup calamondin juice
1   cup heavy cream, whipped
1   prepared 9-inch graham
    cracker crust

Combine condensed milk and juice. Add to whipped cream and mix thoroughly. Pour into pie shell and refrigerate overnight. Makes 1 pie.

Chocolate Cream Pie

1   8-ounce package cream
    cheese
½   cup sugar
1   teaspoon vanilla
3   egg yolks, beaten
1   12-ounce package
    chocolate morsels, melted
    and cooled
3   egg whites, beaten stiff
1   cup heavy cream, whipped
1   prepared 9-inch deep dish
    graham cracker crust

Combine cream cheese, ¼ cup sugar, and vanilla, mixing until smooth. Add egg yolks and beat well. Add chocolate and beat well.

Beat remaining ¼ cup sugar into beaten egg whites. Fold into chocolate mixture. Fold in whipped cream. Pour into crust and freeze. Thaw 20 to 30 minutes before serving. Makes 1 pie.

Peanut Butter Pie

1 3-ounce package cream
   cheese
1 cup confectioners' sugar
⅓ cup smooth peanut butter
¼ cup milk
1 4-ounce container non-
   dairy whipped topping
1 prepared 9-inch graham
   cracker crust
Chopped peanuts, optional
   garnish

Mix cream cheese and confectioners' sugar until well blended. Add peanut butter and milk, mixing well. Fold in whipped topping and pour into pie crust. Refrigerate overnight. Garnish with chopped peanuts, if desired. Makes 1 pie.

Praline Bottom Pumpkin Pie

Crust:
4 tablespoons butter
½ cup chopped pecans,
   toasted
⅓ cup packed brown sugar
1 baked 9-inch pie shell

Melt butter in a small saucepan. Stir in pecans and brown sugar. Cook, stirring over medium heat until mixture bubbles. Spread mixture over bottom of pie shell. Cool.

Filling:
1 2¼ or 3-ounce package no-
   bake custard mix
⅓ cup sugar
2 teaspoons pumpkin pie
   spice
⅔ cup milk
1 5⅓-ounce can evaporated
   milk
1 16-ounce can pumpkin
Whipped cream topping,
   optional garnish

Combine custard mix, sugar, and spice in a 2-quart saucepan. Stir in milk, evaporated milk, and pumpkin. Cook, stirring until mixture bubbles. Cover and cool for 10 minutes. Pour into pie shell and chill until firm. Top with whipped cream, if desired. Makes 1 pie.

Coconut Cream Pie with Almond Crumb Crust

Crust:
1½ cups vanilla wafer crumbs
½   cup finely ground,
     blanched almonds
¼   cup brown sugar, packed
¼   teaspoon nutmeg
⅓   cup melted butter
¼   teaspoon almond extract

Combine all ingredients and pat mixture evenly onto bottom and sides of a 9-inch greased pie pan. Bake at 400 degrees for 8 minutes or until lightly browned. Cool.

Filling:
2   cups milk
½   cup sugar
¼   cup plus 1 tablespoon
     cornstarch
½   teaspoon salt
2   egg yolks, beaten
1   tablespoon vanilla
1   tablespoon butter
1   cup shredded or flaked
     coconut

Heat milk in a large saucepan until it coats the back of a wooden spoon. Mix together the sugar, cornstarch, and salt in a separate bowl. Slowly add the dry ingredients to the heated milk. Cook just until thickened, stirring constantly. Remove from heat. Add egg yolks, beating constantly. Add vanilla, butter, and coconut. Return to stove and cook over medium heat 3 to 4 minutes, stirring regularly. Pour into pie shell.

Topping:
2   cups heavy cream
1   teaspoon vanilla
1   teaspoon sugar

Combine ingredients and whip. Spread over filling. Makes 1 pie.

Upside Down Strawberry Meringue Pie

3   egg whites
½   teaspoon vinegar
¼   teaspoon salt
½   cup sugar
½   teaspoon vanilla
1   baked 9-inch pie shell
3   cups fresh strawberries,
     stems removed
⅓   cup sugar
2   tablespoon cornstarch
½   cup water
Red food coloring
1   cup heavy cream, whipped

Beat egg whites with vinegar and salt to soft peaks. Gradually add ½ cup sugar and vanilla, beating to stiff peaks. Spread on bottom and sides of pie shell. Bake at 325 degrees for 12 minutes. Cool.

Mash and sieve 2 cups of strawberries. Blend together, in a saucepan, ⅓ cup sugar and cornstarch. Add water and mashed berries. Cook and stir 2 minutes until mixture thickens and boils. Tint with several drops red food coloring. Cool slightly. Spread over meringue and chill until set.

Spread whipped cream over pie. Carefully slice remaining berries into fan shapes to garnish top of pie. Makes 1 pie.

Paper Bag Apple Pie

5 to 6 large Jonathan apples
½   cup sugar
2   tablespoons all-purpose
     flour
¼   teaspoon nutmeg
1   unbaked 9-inch deep-dish
     pie shell

Peel, core and cube apples.

Mix together sugar, flour and nutmeg in a bowl. Add apple cubes. Pour into pie shell.

Topping:
½   cup brown sugar
½   cup all-purpose flour
½   cup butter

Cream brown sugar, flour, and butter. Crumble mixture over apple filling.

Place pie in a large brown paper bag, and fasten shut with paper clips or staples. Place bag on a cookie sheet. Bake at 400 degrees for 1 hour. Tear open bag to cool. Makes 1 pie.

Frozen Coffee Pie

Crust:
1   **egg white**
¼ **cup sugar**
1   **cup chopped nuts**

Beat egg white until foamy. Mix in sugar and nuts. Spread mixture over bottom and sides of a 9-inch pie pan. Bake at 350 degrees for 10 to 12 minutes. Cool.

Filling:
¼ **cup milk**
20 **large marshmallows**
1   **heaping teaspoon instant coffee**
1   **cup heavy cream, whipped**
1   **egg yolk**

Heat milk in a saucepan. Add marshmallows and stir until melted. Add coffee and whipped cream. Pour mixture into pie shell and freeze. Makes 1 pie.

Deluxe Key Lime Pie

4   **eggs, separated**
2   **8-ounce cans sweetened condensed milk**
1   **cup key lime juice**
Grated rind of 2 limes
Pinch of salt
1   **prepared 9-inch graham cracker crust**

Beat egg yolks and slowly add milk, lime juice, and grated rind. Whip egg whites with a pinch of salt until stiff, and fold into lime mixture in 3 or 4 batches.

Pour half of mixture into pie crust and place in freezer for 20 minutes, meanwhile refrigerating remaining mixture.

Pour rest of mixture over frozen portion and freeze.

Makes 1 pie.

Florida Sunshine Pie

Crust:

1¼ cups coconut cookie
    crumbs
¼ cup sugar
¼ cup butter or margarine,
    melted

Combine all ingredients and press crumb mixture firmly onto bottom and sides of a 9-inch pie plate. Bake at 350 degrees for 5 to 7 minutes. Cool.

Filling:

1   envelope unflavored
    gelatin
½ cup sugar
¼ teaspoon salt
2   eggs, separated
¾ cup cold water
1   6-ounce can frozen orange
    juice concentrate
1   cup heavy cream, whipped

Combine gelatin with ¼ cup sugar and the salt in a saucepan. Beat together egg yolks and water and add to gelatin. Cook over low heat, stirring constantly, until mixture thickens. Remove from heat and add frozen juice, stirring to dissolve. Chill until mixture mounds.

Beat egg whites until stiff and add remaining ¼ cup sugar, beating to form peaks. Fold into gelatin mixture. Fold in whipped cream. Spoon into pie crust and refrigerate. Makes 1 pie.

Black Bottom Cake

1½ cups all-purpose flour
¼   cup cocoa
½   teaspoon salt
1   cup sugar
1   teaspoon baking soda
1   cup water
⅓   cup vegetable oil
1   tablespoon vinegar
1   teaspoon vanilla
1   8-ounce package cream
    cheese
⅓   cup sugar
1   cup chocolate morsels
1   egg
¼   teaspoon salt
Sifted confectioners' sugar
½   cup chopped almonds

Sift together flour, cocoa, ½ teaspoon salt, 1 cup sugar, and baking soda. Add water, oil, vinegar, and vanilla. Beat until well blended. Pour into a greased 8 x 11-inch pan.

Combine cream cheese, ⅓ cup sugar, chocolate morsels, egg, and ¼ teaspoon salt. Drop by teaspoonfuls onto cake batter. Swirl in with a knife. Bake at 350 degrees for 35 to 40 minutes. Sprinkle top of cake with confectioners' sugar and almonds. Makes 1 cake.

Holiday Lemon Cake

2   cups butter
2⅓ cups sugar
6   eggs
2   ounces lemon extract
4   cups sifted all-purpose
    flour
1½ teaspoons baking powder
½   teaspoon salt
½   pound candied cherries
¼   pound candied pineapple
¾   cup white raisins
4   cups chopped pecans

Cream butter and sugar in a large bowl. Add eggs. Stir in lemon extract.

Sift together flour, baking powder, and salt and add to creamed mixture. Stir in fruit and pecans. Pour into 2 well-greased 9 x 5-inch loaf pans. Bake at 300 degrees for 1½ hours or until done. Cool completely before removing from pan. Makes 2 loaf cakes.

Sunshine Butter Cake and Fresh Coconut Frosting

Cake:

1   cup butter
2   cups sugar
1½ teaspoons vanilla
4   eggs
4   cups cake flour
4   teaspoons baking powder
1   teaspoon salt
1⅓ cups milk

Cream thoroughly the butter and sugar. Add vanilla. Add eggs, one at a time, beating well after each addition. Sift together flour, baking powder, and salt and add to mixture, alternating with milk, ending with flour.

Pour into 3 greased and floured 9-inch cake pans. Bake at 350 degrees for 30 to 40 minutes. Cool 10 minutes before removing from pans. Cool before frosting. Store in cool place or refrigerate. Makes 1 cake.

Frosting:

3   cups sugar
¼   teaspoon cream of tartar
1   cup boiling water
3   egg whites
¾   teaspoon vanilla
½   teaspoon almond flavoring
1   fresh coconut, grated

Combine sugar, cream of tartar, and boiling water in a 3-quart saucepan. With the aid of a candy thermometer that doesn't touch bottom of the pan, cook until mixture reaches 240 degrees and makes a long thread with a spoon. Turn to a low heat when mixture begins to boil. The longer mixture cooks the less likely it is to be grainy.

Beat egg whites in a large bowl until stiff, but not dry. Slowly pour the hot syrup, in a fine stream, into the egg whites, beating constantly. Add vanilla and almond flavoring, and beat until frosting is cool enough to spread. Spread on tops and sides of cake layers, sprinkling with coconut. Join layers together.

Carrot Cake

3	cups sifted cake flour
2	cups sugar
2	teaspoons cinnamon
1½	teaspoons baking soda
1	teaspoon baking powder
1½	teaspoons salt
1	8¾-ounce can crushed pineapple, drained, syrup reserved
3	eggs, beaten
1½	cups vegetable oil
2	teaspoons vanilla
2	cups grated carrots
1½	cups finely chopped nuts

Combine flour, sugar, cinnamon, baking soda, baking powder, and salt in a large bowl. Add pineapple syrup to dry mixture. Add eggs, oil, and vanilla and beat for 3-minutes. Stir in pineapple, carrots, and nuts. Pour into a greased and lightly floured 10-inch tube pan. Bake at 325 degrees for 1½ hours. Cool on rack for 10 minutes before removing from pan. Makes 1 cake.

Rum Cake

1	10-inch angel food cake

Slice angel food cake horizontally into 3 layers. Spread layers with filling. Press layers together and ice cake with whipped cream. Refrigerate. Makes 1 cake.

Filling:

1	cup sweet butter
1	cup sugar
3	eggs
3	tablespoons rum
3	tablespoons bourbon

Cream thoroughly the butter and sugar. Add eggs, one at a time, mixing well. Stir in rum and bourbon. Filling will be runny.

Topping:

2	cups heavy cream, whipped

Banana Cake

Cake:
1½ cups sifted all-purpose
    flour
1   teaspoon baking soda
¼   teaspoon salt
½   cup butter
1   cup sugar
1   teaspoon vanilla
2   eggs
1   cup mashed bananas
¼   cup sour cream

Sift together flour, soda, and salt.

Cream butter, sugar, and vanilla until smooth in a medium-size mixing bowl. Thoroughly beat in the eggs, one at a time. Stir in mashed bananas. Stir in dry, sifted ingredients, alternating with sour cream. Pour into a greased and waxed paper-lined 8 x 8-inch pan. Bake at 350 degrees about 35 minutes. Cool in pan 10 minutes and turn out on a wire rack. Cool before icing. Makes 1 cake.

Icing:
6   tablespoons butter,
    softened
1   8-ounce package cream
    cheese
1   1-pound package
    confectioners' sugar
2   teaspoons vanilla
1   cup chopped pecans

Cream together butter and cream cheese until smooth. Add confectioners' sugar, beating until light and fluffy. Stir in vanilla and pecans.

Chocolate Chip Cake

1   18½-ounce package yellow
    cake mix
1   4⅛-ounce instant
    chocolate pudding
2   6-ounce packages
    chocolate morsels
1   cup water
4   eggs
½   cup vegetable oil

Combine all ingredients and blend for 2 minutes. Pour into a greased and floured 10-inch tube pan. Bake at 350 degrees for 45 to 55 minutes. Cool cake before turning out of pan. Makes 1 cake.

Fresh Strawberry Crumb Cake

1	**cup sifted all-purpose flour**
¾	**cup sugar**
½	**teaspoon baking powder**
¼	**teaspoon baking soda**
1	**egg**
⅓	**cup buttermilk**
½	**teaspoon vanilla**
⅓	**cup butter, melted and cooled**
1½	**cups sliced, fresh strawberries**
1	**cup heavy cream, whipped**

Sift together flour, sugar, baking powder, and soda. Beat together egg, buttermilk, and vanilla. Stir in butter. Pour into flour mixture, mixing until smooth.

Spread batter into a buttered 9-inch round cake pan. Cover batter with sliced strawberries and sprinkle with crumb topping. Bake at 375 degrees for 40 to 45 minutes. Serve warm with whipped cream. Serves 8.

Crumb Topping:

½	**cup firmly packed light brown sugar**
2	**tablespoons all-purpose flour**
1	**tablespoon butter**

Combine ingredients.

Rum Nut Cake

Cake:

1	**cup butter, softened**
1½	**cups sugar**
4	**eggs**
1	**teaspoon vanilla**
2	**cups sifted all-purpose flour**
1½	**teaspoons baking powder**
½	**cup milk**
1	**cup chopped pecans**

Cream butter and sugar in a large mixing bowl. Add eggs, one at a time. Add vanilla. Beat in flour and baking powder, carefully alternating with milk. Stir in pecans. Pour into a greased and floured 10-inch tube pan. Bake at 325 degrees for 1 hour. Cool for 5 minutes before removing from pan. Makes 1 cake.

Rum Sauce:

¾	**cup sugar**
¼	**cup plus ⅛ teaspoon rum**
¼	**cup orange juice**

Combine sugar, rum, and orange juice in a saucepan. Boil 1 minute and pour over cake.

Hershey Bar Cake

Cake:
1 cup butter
2 cups sugar
4 eggs
2 5-ounce cans Hershey chocolate syrup
1 teaspoon vanilla
2½ cups sifted all-purpose flour
½ teaspoon salt
½ teaspoon baking powder
½ teaspoon baking soda
1 cup buttermilk
6 1.05-ounce Hershey chocolate candy bars

Cream butter and sugar. Add eggs, one at a time, into butter mixture, beating well. Add chocolate syrup and vanilla.

Sift together flour, salt, baking powder, and soda. Add alternately to chocolate mixture along with buttermilk.

Melt chocolate bars in top of a double boiler and add to mixture. Pour into a greased 10-inch tube cake pan. Bake at 325 degrees for 1 hour and 20 minutes. Cool. Remove cake from pan and pour warm icing over cake. Makes 1 cake.

Icing:
6 1.05-ounce Hershey chocolate candy bars
3 tablespoons milk

Melt chocolate bars and milk in top of a double boiler. Pour over cake.

Applesauce Cake

Cake:
2 cups sugar
1 cup vegetable oil
4 eggs, beaten
2 cups sifted all-purpose flour
2 teaspoons cinnamon
⅛ teaspoon salt
1 20-ounce can applesauce

Combine sugar and oil in a large bowl. Add eggs, flour, soda, cinnamon, and salt and beat well. Add applesauce and beat until well mixed. Pour batter into 3 greased 9-inch cake pans. Bake at 325 degrees for 30 to 35 minutes. Cool before icing. Makes 1 cake.

Icing:
½ cup butter or margarine
1 8-ounce package cream cheese
1 1-pound package confectioners' sugar
2 teaspoons vanilla
1 cup chopped pecans

Cream butter and cream cheese until smooth. Add confectioners' sugar, beating until light and fluffy. Stir in vanilla and pecans.

Calamondin Spice Cake

12 calamondins, peeled,
   seeded, ground to make ¾
   cup
⅓ cup sugar
1⅓ cups sifted all-purpose
   flour
1   teaspoon salt
1   teaspoon baking soda
¼ teaspoon mace
¼ teaspoon ground cloves
½ teaspoon cinnamon
1   egg
⅓ cup vegetable oil
¾ cup brown sugar

Combine calamondins and ⅓ cup sugar in a large bowl.

Sift together flour, salt, baking soda, mace, cloves, and cinnamon. Add to calamondin mixture.

Cream together egg, oil, and brown sugar and add to mixture. Pour into a greased 8 x 8-inch pan. Bake at 350 degrees for 35 minutes. Makes 1 cake.

Brown Sugar Pound Cake

Cake:
1   cup butter
½ cup vegetable oil
1   cup sugar
1   1-pound package light
   brown sugar
5   eggs
3   cups sifted all-purpose
   flour
1   teaspoon baking powder
½ teaspoon salt
1   cup milk
1   teaspoon vanilla
1   cup chopped nuts

Combine butter and oil in a large bowl. Gradually add sugar and brown sugar, creaming until mixture is light and fluffy. Beat in eggs, one at a time. Sift together flour, baking powder, and salt and add to the butter mixture, alternating with milk. Blend in vanilla. Stir in nuts.

Pour into a greased 10-inch tube pan. Bake at 350 degrees for 1 hour and 15 minutes. Cool 10 minutes and remove from pan. Pour glaze over the hot cake and broil until bubbly and lightly browned. Cool. Makes 1 cake.

Glaze:
2   tablespoons vegetable oil
2   tablespoons butter
½ cup brown sugar
½ teaspoon salt
2   tablespoons milk
1   teaspoon vanilla
Chopped nuts

Combine first 5 ingredients in a saucepan and bring to a boil. Remove from heat. Stir in vanilla and desired amount of chopped nuts.

Black Russian Cake

Cake:
1   18½-ounce package
     chocolate cake mix
½   cup vegetable oil
1   4⅛-ounce package instant
     chocolate pudding
4   eggs, at room temperature
¾   cup strong coffee
⅓   cup coffee-flavored liqueur
⅓   cup chocolate-flavored
     liqueur

Combine all ingredients in a large bowl. Beat about 4 minutes at medium speed or until smooth. Pour into a greased 10-inch bundt pan. Bake at 350 degrees for 55 to 60 minutes. Cool before removing from pan. Punch holes in cake with a meat fork, and spoon topping over cake. Makes 1 cake.

Topping:
1   cup sifted confectioners'
     sugar
2   tablespoons strong coffee
2   tablespoons coffee-
     flavored liqueur
2   tablespoons chocolate-
     flavored liqueur

Combine all ingredients, mixing well.

Aunt Moree's Rich Strawberry Shortcake

2   cups all-purpose flour
¼   cup sugar
2   teaspoons baking powder
½   teaspoon salt
⅛   teaspoon nutmeg
⅓   cup butter, softened
1   egg, well beaten
⅓   cup milk
1   pint strawberries, sliced
1   cup heavy cream, whipped

Sift together flour, sugar, baking powder, salt, and nutmeg. Mix in butter. Add egg and milk. Blend together all ingredients. Pour batter into 12 greased muffin tins. Bake at 450 degrees for 20 minutes. Remove from pans and break open muffins.

Pour strawberries over hot cakes, allowing fruit and juice to run inside. Top with whipped cream. Serves 12.

Almond Brittle

1   cup sugar
½   cup light corn syrup
¼   teaspoon salt
¼   cup water
1   cup sliced almonds
2   tablespoons butter
1   teaspoon baking soda

Combine sugar, corn syrup, salt, and water in a heavy, medium size saucepan over medium-high heat. Bring mixture to a boil, stirring until sugar is dissolved. Stir in almonds.

Insert candy thermometer into pan. Continue cooking, stirring regularly to keep mixture from boiling over, until temperature reaches 300 degrees or until a small amount of the mixture, dropped into very cold water, separates into hard brittle threads.

Remove pan from heat and immediately stir in butter and baking soda. Pour at once onto a greased 11 x 15-inch cookie sheet. With 2 forks, lift and pull mixture into a rectangular shape. Cool. Break into small pieces. Store in an air-tight container. Serves 10.

Angie's Fudge

1½ cups sugar
1   tablespoon butter, melted
½   cup evaporated milk
16 marshmallows, cut into
     small pieces
1   12-ounce package semi-
     sweet chocolate morsels
1   cup chopped nuts
1   teaspoon vanilla

Microwave
Combine sugar, butter, and milk in a 2-quart glass mixing bowl. Microwave on medium-high for 2 to 3 minutes until mixture begins to boil. Remove from oven and stir well.

Return bowl to oven and again microwave on medium-high until mixture boils and sugar is completely dissolved. Stir in marshmallows and chocolate morsels and microwave until smooth. Stir in nuts and vanilla. Spread mixture evenly in a buttered 8-inch baking dish or pan. Cool. Cut into 1-inch squares. Makes 5 dozen pieces candy.

Cinnamon Pecans

1   egg white
1   teaspoon water
1   pound pecan halves
½   cup sugar
¼   teaspoon salt
½   teaspoon cinnamon

Beat egg white with water until frothy. Add pecan halves and mix until well coated.

Combine remaining ingredients in a separate bowl. Stir mixture into pecans and coat well. Bake in a greased jelly roll pan at 250 degrees for 1 hour, stirring every 15 minutes. Cool. Store in a tightly sealed container. Makes 4 cups.

Toffee

1   cup butter
1   cup firmly packed brown sugar
35 saltine crackers
1   12-ounce package semi-sweet chocolate morsels

Melt together butter and brown sugar. Place crackers, in a single layer, on a 9 x 11-inch cookie sheet. Pour butter mixture over crackers. Bake at 375 degrees for 15 minutes.

While still hot, sprinkle chocolate morsels over crackers. Let set 5 minutes, then spread the chocolate. Cool. Break apart into chunks. Makes 3 dozen pieces candy.

Truffles

8   1-ounce squares semi-sweet chocolate
¼   cup sifted confectioners' sugar
3   tablespoons butter
3   egg yolks, lightly beaten
1   tablespoon brandy
½   teaspoon cinnamon

Melt 6 squares of chocolate with the confectioners' sugar and butter in the top of a double boiler. Remove from heat. Stir a small amount of chocolate mixture into egg yolks. Slowly stir yolks into remaining chocolate mixture. Stir in brandy. Chill, without stirring, 1 to 2 hours.

Form by ½ teaspoonfuls of mixture into small balls. Grate remaining 2 squares of chocolate and toss with cinnamon. Roll balls in cinnamon mixture. Store in a cool place in airtight containers. Makes 3 to 4 dozen pieces candy.

Bourbon Balls

**40 to 45 vanilla wafer cookies,
crumbled**
2½ cups confectioners' sugar
2 tablespoons cocoa
1 cup chopped pecans
**1½ tablespoons light corn
syrup**
⅓ cup bourbon

Combine cookie crumbs with 1 cup confec-tioners' sugar, cocoa, and nuts. Combine corn syrup and bourbon and add to crumb mixture, mixing well. Shape into small balls and roll balls in remaining confectioners' sugar. Store in an airtight container for several days before serving. Makes 3 to 4 dozen pieces candy.

Best Ever Caramels

1 cup light corn syrup
2 cups sugar
3 cups heavy cream

Combine corn syrup, sugar, and 1 cup cream in a heavy saucepan. Insert a candy ther-mometer and cook, stirring constantly, until mixture reaches 236 degrees. Add 1 more cup of cream and boil to 236 degrees. Add remain-ing 1 cup cream and boil until thermometer reaches 246 degrees. Pour mixture into a well-buttered 9 x 13-inch pan. Cool.

Cut into bite-size squares and wrap each piece in waxed paper. Keep in a covered con-tainer in the refrigerator. Makes 5 dozen pieces candy.

Chocolate Dipped Strawberries

**4 1-ounce squares semi-
sweet chocolate**
**4 1-ounce squares
unsweetened chocolate**
¼ cup butter
¼ cup light corn syrup
1 pint fresh strawberries

Combine chocolates, butter, and corn syrup in a 1-quart saucepan over very low heat, stir-ring until melted and smooth. Remove pan from heat and beat mixture with a wooden spoon until cooled.

Using 2 forks, dip strawberries halfway into chocolate. Set strawberries on waxed paper to cool. Refrigerate. When chocolate is hard-ened, store candy in a covered container in refrigerator. Makes 1⅓ cups chocolate coating.

Buttercreams

1   1-pound package
    confectioners' sugar
1   cup butter, room
    temperature
2½ teaspoons vanilla
1   teaspoon almond extract
Dash salt
7   1-ounce squares semi-
    sweet chocolate
2   tablespoons paraffin

Combine all ingredients together with hands until creamy and smooth. Refrigerate 45 minutes, or until mixture is hard enough to roll into small bite-sized balls. Refrigerate balls.

Melt chocolate with paraffin. Insert toothpicks into balls and dip into chocolate mixture. Place balls on waxed paper. Refrigerate. Makes about 5 dozen pieces candy.

Washington Brownies

¾ cup sugar
¾ cup brown sugar
1   cup butter or margarine,
    softened
2   eggs
1½ cups all-purpose flour
1   teaspoon salt
1   teaspoon baking soda
1   teaspoon vanilla
2   cups uncooked oats
1   12-ounce package semi-
    sweet chocolate morsels
1   cup chopped walnuts
Confectioners' sugar

Cream sugars and butter or margarine together in a large bowl. Add eggs and mix well.
Mix in flour, salt, baking soda, and vanilla.
Gently stir in the oats, chocolate morsels, and
walnuts. Pat mixture into a greased 9 x 13-
inch pan. Bake at 350 degrees for 20 to 25
minutes. Sprinkle with confectioners' sugar.
Makes 2½ dozen.

Addie's Chocolate Cookies

Cookies:
½ cup butter, melted
1   cup brown sugar
2   1-ounce squares semi-
    sweet chocolate, melted
1⅓ cups all-purpose flour
½ teaspoon baking soda
1   egg, separated
½ cup milk
1   cup chopped nuts

Combine butter, brown sugar, and melted
chocolate, mixing well.

Combine flour and baking soda. Beat egg
yolk and milk together with a fork. Add the
flour mixture to the chocolate mixture in 4
stages, alternating with the egg mixture. Stir
in nuts.

Beat egg white and fold into the cookie
dough. Drop by heaping teaspoonfuls onto
greased cookie sheets. Bake at 350 degrees
for 8 minutes. Cookies will be cakelike. Cool.

Frosting:
4   1-ounce squares semi-
    sweet chocolate, melted
4   tablespoons butter
2   cups confectioners' sugar
4   tablespoons light cream

Combine melted chocolate and butter.
Gradually add confectioners' sugar. Add
cream, blending until smooth. Spread on
cooled cookies. Makes 4 dozen.

Shortbread

1   **cup butter**
¾   **cup sugar**
2   **cups plus 2 tablespoons**
     all-purpose flour
½   **cup cornstarch**
¼   **teaspoon salt**

Cream butter and sugar. Add flour, corn-starch, and salt, using all bits of flour, kneading mixture well. Roll dough out to ½-inch thick on a lightly floured surface. Cut into squares or shapes and place on a greased cookie sheet. Prick each square well with a fork. Chill ½ hour.

Bake at 375 degrees for 5 minutes. Reduce heat to 300 degrees. Continue baking for about 20 minutes, until delicately brown, watching carefully. Makes 3½ dozen.

Chocolate Almond Meringues

1   **6-ounce package semi-**
     sweet chocolate morsels
3   **egg whites**
½   **teaspoon vanilla**
1   **cup sugar**
⅓   **cup finely chopped**
     almonds

Melt chocolate morsels in top of a double boiler. Cool 5 minutes. Beat egg whites and vanilla together until soft peaks form. Gradually add sugar and beat until very stiff. Fold in almonds and the melted, cooled chocolate.

Drop by teaspoonfuls onto greased cookie sheets. Bake at 350 degrees for 10 to 12 minutes. Makes 4 dozen.

Pecan Fruit Christmas Cookies

¾   **cup butter**
1   **cup sugar**
1   **egg, separated**
1   **cup all-purpose flour**
1   **cup chopped pecans**
2   **candied pineapple rings,**
     diced
3   **ounces candied red and**
     green cherries, diced

Cream butter and sugar until light and fluffy. Add egg yolk, blending well; add flour. Beat egg white until stiff and fold into batter. Stir in nuts and fruit. Drop by teaspoonfuls on a foil-lined cookie sheet.

Bake at 350 degrees 8 to 12 minutes. Edges will be brown, centers lighter. Cool on foil and then peel off. Makes 3 to 4 dozen.

Pumpkin Faces

¼   cup butter
⅔   cup brown sugar
½   cup pumpkin
¾   cup light molasses
3   cups all-purpose flour
1   tablespoon baking soda
½   teaspoon salt
½   teaspoon each of ginger,
    cinnamon, nutmeg, allspice
1   .68-ounce tube brown
    decorating gel
1   .68-ounce tube green
    decorating gel

Cream butter and sugar. Stir in pumpkin and molasses. Sift together the flour, baking soda, salt, and spices and blend into the pumpkin mixture. Cover and chill 2 to 3 hours.

Roll dough ¼-inch thick on a lightly floured surface. Cut with a pumpkin-shaped cookie cutter, and carefully place cookies on greased cookie sheets.

Bake at 375 degrees for 8 to 10 minutes. Cool. Decorate with drawn mouths and eyes of brown gel and stems of green gel. Makes 2 dozen.

Swedish Creams

Cookies:
1   cup butter
⅓   cup heavy cream
2   cups all-purpose flour
Sugar

Mix butter, cream and flour together. Chill. Roll out dough to ⅛-inch thick on a lightly floured surface. Cut into 1½-inch circles.

Dip circles in sugar, place on a cookie sheet, and prick each circle 3 times with a fork. Bake at 375 degrees for 6 minutes or until lightly browned. Cool.

Filling:
¼   cup butter
1   cup confectioners' sugar
1   teaspoon cream
Food coloring of choice

Combine ingredients. Spread filling between 2 baked circles, sandwich style, to form cookies. Makes 3 to 4 dozen.

Pecan Macaroons

6   egg whites
¼   cup all-purpose flour
1   16-ounce package
    confectioners' sugar
4   cups finely chopped pecans
1   teaspoon vanilla

Beat egg whites until stiff. Sprinkle flour on top of egg whites and gradually beat in, along with the sugar. Fold in chopped nuts and vanilla. Drop by rounded teaspoonfuls onto a brown paper-lined cookie sheet, 1½-inches apart. Bake at 350 degrees for 20 minutes. Makes 4 dozen.

Yummy Cookies

1   cup butter
1   cup vegetable oil
1   cup brown sugar
1   cup sugar
1   egg
1   teaspoon almond extract
1   teaspoon vanilla
3¾ cups all-purpose flour
1   teaspoon baking soda
1   teaspoon cream of tartar
1   cup uncooked oatmeal
1   cup rice crispies cereal
½   cup chopped nuts

Cream butter, oil, and sugars. Add egg, almond extract, and vanilla. Sift together the flour, baking soda, and cream of tartar. Add to the butter mixture and blend. Add remaining ingredients.

Shape into balls the size of small walnuts and place on a greased cookie sheet. Flatten balls with a fork or a floured glass bottom. Bake at 350 degrees for 12 to 15 minutes. Makes 12 to 15 dozen.

Gooey Butter Cake Bars

1   18½-ounce package yellow, butter-flavored, cake mix
3   eggs
½   cup chopped nuts
¾   cup flaked coconut
½   cup butter or margarine, softened
1   8-ounce package cream cheese
1   16-ounce package confectioners' sugar

Combine cake mix, 1 egg, nuts, coconut, and butter. Spread into bottom and sides of a 9 x 13-inch baking pan.

Combine cream cheese, 2 eggs, and confectioners' sugar. Beat 5 minutes. Pour over cake mixture. Bake at 350 degrees for 30 to 35 minutes, until top starts to brown. Cool. Refrigerate. Cut into squares. Makes 2½ to 3 dozen bars.

Texas Bars

4   eggs, beaten
1   1-pound package light brown sugar
2   cups Bisquick
1   teaspoon vanilla
½   teaspoon salt
2   cups chopped nuts

Cream together eggs and sugar in a large bowl. Add remaining ingredients. Spread thinly on a 10 x 15-inch cookie sheet. Bake at 300 degrees for 40 to 45 minutes. Cool and cut into bars. Makes 7 dozen bars.

Chocolate Mint Squares

Cake Layer:
½   **cup butter, softened**
1   **cup sugar**
2   **eggs**
½   **cup all-purpose flour**
2   **1-ounce squares
    unsweetened chocolate,
    melted**
½   **cup chopped pecans**

Cream butter and sugar until light and fluffy. Add eggs and beat thoroughly. Add flour and blend well. Add chocolate, blending thoroughly; stir in pecans. Pour into a greased 9 x 9-inch pan. Bake at 350 degrees for 20 minutes. Cool in pan.

Peppermint Filling:
1   **tablespoon butter, softened**
1   **cup confectioners' sugar**
2   **tablespoons crème de
    menthe**

Blend butter and sugar. Stir in crème de menthe until of spreading consistency. Spread filling over cake layer. Refrigerate.

Chocolate Glaze:
2   **1-ounce squares semi-
    sweet chocolate**
1   **tablespoon butter**

Melt chocolate and butter, stirring well. Spread glaze over cold peppermint filling. Chill. Cut into 1-inch squares. Store in refrigerator. Makes 4 dozen.

Peanut Butter Fingers

Cookies:
3   **cups rice crispies cereal,
    coarsely crushed**
½   **cup butter**
2   **cups crunchy peanut butter**
1   **16-ounce package
    confectioners' sugar**
1   **teaspoon vanilla**

Combine all ingredients in a large bowl, mixing well with hands, and form into 1 x 1½-inch long fingers or into 1-inch balls. Chill.

Glaze:
1   **12-ounce package semi-
    sweet chocolate morsels**
¼   **pound paraffin**

Melt chocolate morsels and paraffin together. Dip cookies into the mixture and place on waxed paper to cool. Store in refrigerator. Makes about 6 dozen.

Half Way Bars

1	cup butter or margarine
½	cup sugar
1½	cups brown sugar
2	eggs, separated
1	tablespoon water
½	teaspoon vanilla
2	cups sifted all-purpose flour
¼	teaspoon salt
1	tablespoon baking powder
¼	teaspoon baking soda
1	6-ounce package chocolate morsels
1	6-ounce package butterscotch morsels

Cream together the butter, sugar and ½ cup brown sugar. Add egg yolks, water, and vanilla.

Sift together 3 separate times, the flour, salt, baking powder, and soda. Mix into the egg and sugar mixture. Spread onto a greased 10 x 15-inch jelly roll pan. Sprinkle chocolate morsels over ½ of the batter and sprinkle butterscotch morsels over the other half.

Beat egg whites until stiff. Gradually fold in 1 cup brown sugar. Spread over the morsels. Bake at 350 degrees for 20 minutes. Cool. Cut into bars. Makes 5 dozen.

French Pastry Squares

Crust:

1	cup all-purpose flour
¼	cup brown sugar
⅓	cup butter

Combine all ingredients. Press mixture into an ungreased 9 x 9-inch pan. Bake at 350 degrees for 10 minutes.

Topping:

2	eggs
1	cup coconut
1	cup chopped pecans
2	tablespoons all-purpose flour
1	teaspoon vanilla
1	teaspoon baking powder
1½	cups brown sugar

Combine all ingredients in a large bowl, mixing well. Spread over the baked crust, return to oven, and bake 30 to 40 minutes until firm. Cut into squares. Makes 25.

Ting-a-Lings

1	12-ounce package butterscotch morsels
1	5-ounce can chow mein noodles
½	cup chopped peanuts

Melt butterscotch morsels in top of a double boiler. Add noodles and peanuts and stir to coat well. Drop by teaspoonfuls onto waxed paper lined cookie sheets. Chill. Makes 3 to 4 dozen.

Cherrybims

1   cup butter or margarine
⅔   cup sugar
1   egg
½   teaspoon vanilla
¼   teaspoon almond extract
1¾ cups all-purpose flour, sifted
½   teaspoon salt
⅓   cup finely chopped, well drained, maraschino cherries

Cream butter and sugar until light and fluffy. Add egg, vanilla and almond extract, beating well. Add flour, salt, and cherries; mix thoroughly. Refrigerate overnight.

Drop by teaspoonfuls onto ungreased cookie sheets about 2-inches apart. Bake at 400 degrees for 10 minutes or until lightly browned. Makes 3 dozen.

Tricolor Pinwheels

2½ cups all-purpose flour
1½ cups sugar
1   cup butter, softened
1   egg
1½ teaspoons baking powder
1   teaspoon vanilla
½   teaspoon salt
7 to 8 drops red food coloring
7 to 8 drops green food coloring
Confectioners' sugar

Combine the first 7 ingredients in a large bowl. Beat with a mixer at low speed for about 3 minutes until smooth. Divide dough into 3 equal parts. Mix red food coloring into one third, green food coloring into another third, and leave the remaining third plain. Cover doughs and refrigerate 2 hours.

Divide each dough third in half, making 6 equal parts.

In confectioners' sugar, roll out a green dough portion on waxed paper to form a 10 x 6-inch rectangle. Separately roll out the red and plain doughs to the same dimension. Invert plain dough rectangle on top of green dough and peel off the waxed paper. Invert red dough on top of the plain dough so the 3 rectangles are stacked on top of one another.

Starting at one long side, roll dough tightly, jellyroll fashion, peeling back the waxed paper on the bottom while rolling. Repeat complete procedure with remaining portions of dough. Wrap rolls and refrigerate overnight.

Slice each roll crosswise into ¼-inch slices. Place slices on lightly greased cookie sheets, 1 inch apart. Bake at 350 degrees for 12 minutes. Cool. Store in airtight containers. Makes 80.

Daddy's Mint Julep Syrup

2   cups sugar
2   cups water
1   large bunch fresh mint

Boil sugar and water mixture and pour over mint. Let sit in refrigerator for at least 2 days. One tablespoon syrup, plus 1 jigger of bourbon, served over crushed ice, makes the traditional Kentucky Mint Julep. Makes about 1-quart mint julep syrup.

Claret Cup

2   lemons, sliced
1   cup cold water
½   cup sugar
4   cups dry red wine, chilled
2   cups champagne, chilled
1   cup dry sherry, chilled

Place sliced lemons in a punch bowl, 1 hour before serving. Add cold water and sugar and stir. Just before serving, add wines. Serves 20.

Hot Spiced Punch

¾   teaspoon whole cloves
2   cups orange juice
Juice of 1 lemon
¾   cup sugar
1   3-inch stick cinnamon
1   teaspoon grated orange
    rind
2   cups water
1   small tea bag
1   orange, sliced
¼   teaspoon whole cloves

Put cloves in a cheesecloth bag and combine with fruit juices, sugar, cinnamon, orange rind, and water. Simmer for 5 minutes. Add tea bag and allow to stand several minutes. Strain and pour into a heated pitcher. Stud orange slices with ¼ teaspoon cloves and float on top of punch. Serves 6.

Seagrape Juice

1   quart seagrapes
2½ quarts water
2 to 3 cups sugar

Put seagrapes into a large kettle. Add 1½-quarts water. Cook, covered, until pulp and skin slips from the stones when pressed, usually about 25 minutes. Strain grapes through several layers of cheesecloth, without pressing.

To the remaining seeds and pulp, add remaining 1-quart water and cook for 15 minutes more. Strain.

To prepare juice, add sugar and boil for 5 minutes. Pour into sterilized jars and seal This juice may be used as is or combined with other fruit juices for a punch. Makes about 3 quarts.

Frozen Margaritas

1   6-ounce can limeade
    concentrate, frozen
6   ounces tequila
3   ounces triple sec
12 to 16 ice cubes
1   lime, cut into wedges
Coarse salt

Put frozen limeade, tequila, and triple sec in blender and mix for 5 seconds. With machine running, add ice cubes, 2 at a time. Continuing to add cubes until mixture becomes a thick slush.

Rub rims of glasses with a lime wedge then dip into salt. Pour lime mixture into glasses and serve. Makes 4 to 5 cups.

Fresh Lemonade

Syrup Base:
1   tablespoon fresh, grated
    lemon rind
1½ cups sugar
½   cup boiling water
1½ cups fresh squeezed lemon
    juice

Combine lemon rind, sugar, and boiling water in a jar. Cover and shake until sugar dissolves. Add lemon juice. Store tightly covered in refrigerator. Makes 2⅔ cups syrup base.

Lemonade:
2⅔ cups lemonade syrup base
5   cups cold water

Combine syrup with cold water in a large pitcher and stir. Makes 1¾ quarts.

Iced Tea Punch

1   cup sugar
4   cups strong tea
4   cups lemonade
4   cups orange juice
1   cup pineapple juice
Fresh mint, for garnish

Dissolve sugar into tea. Pour into a gallon container and add lemonade, orange, and pineapple juices, mixing well. Garnish each serving with a sprig of mint. Makes 1 gallon.

Cranberry Flip

2   cups cranberry juice
2   cups orange juice
1   egg
1   cup gin or vodka, optional

Place all ingredients in a blender. Blend a few seconds until foamy. Serves 6 to 8.

Orange Frosty

1   cup orange juice
2   tablespoons honey
1   pint vanilla ice cream

Combine orange juice and honey in a blender. Add ice cream, a little at a time, blending until creamy. Pour into tall chilled glasses. Serves 2.

Picnic Bloody Marys

1   46-ounce can tomato juice
4   tablespoons fresh lemon juice
1   tablespoon horseradish
2   tablespoons Worcestershire sauce
1   tablespoon salt
Few drops Tabasco
2   cups vodka
Celery sticks

Combine all ingredients and chill overnight in a covered container. Will keep, refrigerated, for 1 week. Garnish each serving with celery sticks. Serves 8 to 10.

Fish House Punch

Juice of 6 lemons
2　cups confectioners' sugar
½　pint brandy
¼　pint peach brandy
¼　pint Jamaican rum
3　32-ounce bottles club soda

Combine all ingredients and stir. Pour over ice ring in a large punch bowl. Makes 42 ½-cup servings.

Sangria

1　25.4-ounce bottle red wine
1　28-ounce bottle tonic
　　water
½　cup sugar
1　sliced orange
1　sliced lemon
1　sliced peach
1　sliced banana, optional

Combine all ingredients and mix well. Serve cold. Serves 10.

Hot Spiced Wine

1　25.4-ounce bottle
　　Beaujolais
¼　cup lemon juice
1　cup port wine
¼　teaspoon ground ginger
¼　teaspoon whole cloves
1　cinnamon stick, broken
　　into pieces
¼　cup sugar

Combine all ingredients and heat. Serves 6.

Champagne Punch

2 cups sugar
2 cups fresh lemon juice
5 cups fresh orange juice
2 4/5 bottles sauterne, chilled
1 25.4-ounce bottle champagne, chilled
1 lemon, sliced
1 orange, sliced

Combine sugar and fruit juices and stir until sugar dissolves. Chill. Just before serving, place a small ring of ice in a punch bowl, and pour in sauterne. Add champagne and garnish with fruit slices. Serves 24.

Mincemeat Glazed Apples

1 3-ounce package cherry-flavored gelatin
1 3-ounce package orange-flavored gelatin
1½ cups boiling water
1 cup cold water
6 baking apples
1 cup prepared mincemeat

Dissolve gelatins in boiling water. Add cold water.

Pare apples, and cut a 1-inch deep cavity into center top of each. Place apples with open end up, in a large skillet. Fill centers with mincemeat. Pour gelatin mixture over apples and bring to a boil over medium heat. Cover pan and reduce heat. Simmer 15 minutes or until tender. Remove cover and place apples under broiler for 10 to 15 minutes, watching carefully. Serves 6.

Sweet Spiced Kumquats

1 quart kumquats
Water
3 cups sugar
1 cup vinegar
3 cups water
1 tablespoon whole pickling spices

Make a small slit, crosswise, in each kumquat. Cover fruit with water in a saucepan and bring to a boil. Cook 10 minutes. Drain.

Make a syrup of sugar, vinegar, and 3 cups water. Bring to a boil and drop in spices tied in a small, clean cloth. Cook 5 minutes.

Let fruit stand overnight in syrup to plump. Bring syrup to a boil and cook until thick. Pack fruit into jars and cover with hot syrup. Seal and adjust lids. Process in boiling water-bath canner for 10 minutes.

Orange-Lemon-Carrot Marmalade

2 oranges, juiced
Water
4 cups sugar
3 cups cooked, mashed
   carrots
2 lemons, juiced
1 cup water

Chop orange rind into small pieces and boil, covered with water, until tender. Discard water.

Pour sugar over hot mashed carrots and allow to melt. Add juices of oranges and lemons, orange rind, and 1 cup water and mix well. Cook for about 45 minutes until mixture is thick and clear. Cool several minutes.

Pour into clean, hot jars, leaving ½-inch head space. Adjust lids and process in boiling water-bath canner for 10 minutes, if long storage is desired.

Crystallized Citrus Peel

2 cups thick fruit peel, cut
   into ¼ to ½-inch wide
   strips
2 quarts water
⅔ cup corn syrup
1⅓ cups sugar
1⅓ cups water
½ teaspoon salt
Sugar

Simmer strips of peel for 30 minutes in 2 quarts water, adding more water as necessary. Discard water. Add fresh water and repeat procedure twice.

Combine corn syrup, 1⅓ cups water, and salt in a saucepan. Bring to a boil. Add fruit peel, and boil gently for 30 minutes. Reduce heat and cook slowly 30 to 40 minutes or until all syrup has been absorbed. Roll peel in granulated sugar. Place on rack to cool.

Package peel in airtight containers and freeze for long storage, or store in boxes, lined with waxed paper, or in jars with a few air holes in the lid. Peel will keep 2 or 3 months. Serve as candy or where candied fruit is used in recipes.

Spicy Breakfast Peaches

½ cup sugar
½ cup water
⅓ cup red cinnamon candies
1 lemon, thinly sliced
1 1-pound, 13-ounce can
   cling peach halves, drained

Combine sugar, water, cinnamon candies, and lemon slices in a saucepan. Bring to a boil and simmer 5 minutes, or until candy dissolves. Add peach halves. Simmer 5 to 8 minutes. Serve hot. Serves 4 to 6.

Holiday Fruit Compote

4   oranges
1   papaya
1   pineapple
2½ cups seedless green grapes
1   cup marsala wine
¾ cup sugar
1   cinnamon stick
3   whole cloves

Cut 3 strips of rind from 1 orange and reserve. Peel oranges and slice crossways.

Pare papaya, cut in half lengthwise, and remove seeds. Cut into cubes.

Remove rind from pineapple. Cut pineapple into lengthwise quarters. Core and cut pineapple into 2-inch long strips.

Combine oranges, papaya, pineapple and grapes in a large bowl.

Combine wine, sugar, cinnamon stick, cloves, and orange rind in a saucepan. Stir over medium heat until sugar dissolves. Reduce heat and simmer 5 minutes. Remove spices and rind. Cool syrup to lukewarm, and pour over fruit in the bowl. Cover and refrigerate overnight. Can be served warm or cold. Serves 8 to 10.

Candied Kumquats–Dried

1   quart kumquats
1   tablespoon baking soda
Water
2½ cups sugar
2   cups water
½ cup corn syrup

Sprinkle kumquats with baking soda. Cover with water and let soak in the soda solution 20 minutes. Drain, rinse in several changes of cold water. Make a slit in each kumquat, through to the seeds.

Dissolve 2 cups of the sugar in 2 cups water and bring to a boil. Add kumquats and simmer 30 minutes. Remove from heat, weight the fruit down with a plate to keep it submerged, and let cool, and plump for 24 hours.

Drain off the syrup and add it to remaining ½ cup of sugar and the corn syrup. Bring to a boil and simmer until kumquats are plump and transparent. Again submerge the fruit in the syrup and let it plump for 24 hours. Reheat kumquats in syrup, boil for 30 minutes, and cool.

Lift kumquats from syrup and place on racks to dry in sun or in a cool oven, 100 degrees. The kumquats may then be stuffed with fondant or nutmeats and rolled in granulated sugar, or dipped in glaze.

TROPICAL FRUITS

Tropical Fruits

The three major tropical fruits of South Florida are citrus, mango, and avocado, the latter being more commonly used as a vegetable rather than a fruit. These three are fairly well-known throughout the country because their taste is appealing to many people and also because they are on the market in large amounts.

The following list includes our favorite and most abundant fruits of whose existence all of which our northern friends may not be aware. These delicacies can be prepared in a wide variety of ways or, in most cases, may be eaten in their natural state. We hope you'll be able to acquire these delights and enjoy them as we in the Palm Beaches do.

Tropical Fruits
Avocado

1 cup equals 190 calories

Avocados come in different shapes, sizes, and a variety of green shades. There are 67 Florida avocado varieties, generally available in the cooler months. All have a delicate nutlike flavor and a smooth creamy texture. Florida avocados are lower in calories than any others domestically grown, and many claim they are superior in taste.

Avocados are handpicked from the tree when mature but are "eating ripe" at a later period when they have lost their feeling of firmness and yield to gentle pressure of the hand. To speed ripening, place avocado in a brown paper bag.

To split an avocado in half, simply cut lengthwise around the seed. Turn halves in opposite directions to separate. Lift out the seed and peel skin off the avocado with knife or fingers. To prevent discoloration if you're not using it right away, sprinkle cut surface with lemon or lime juice, leave the seed in place, and cover the avocado with plastic or foil. Ripe avocados, whole or cut, can be stored in the refrigerator for several days. However, cooking at high temperatures is not advised as avocados contain tannin and will develop a very bitter flavor.

Suggested Uses:

Salads are the favorite way of serving avocados. The flavor combines well with acid fruits and vegetables and with vinegar and other tart salad dressings. Avocados are the main ingredient in guacamole, and many people like them split and stuffed with crab or chicken salad. Or for the purist, sliced avocado with salt and pepper is heaven itself.

Whole or sliced avocados do not freeze well. However, they may be frozen in a puree form.

Banana

1 medium banana equals 101 calories

The banana was probably among the first crop plants of primitive man. Today it is one of the most important and widely grown of tropical fruits with roughly 300 varieties in existence.

Bananas are divided into two main types: sweet eating bananas and cooking bananas, known as plantains. For the people of the tropics the plantain replaces the potato. This fruit is larger than the sweet banana, the skin is stiff and thick and clings tightly to the fruit. It is a deeper yellow in color, and the fruit tapers sharply at base and tip.

Bananas have many uses, depending on the type. They are good raw, cooked, baked, broiled, boiled, or frozen. They may be used in a large variety of beverages, entrees, breads, salads and desserts.

The banana is sanitarily sealed by nature in a dust-proof easily opened wrapper. The best stage for eating a banana is when the skin begins to show spotting. A partly ripe fruit is very indigestible when uncooked. When fully ripe, practically all the starch of the banana has been converted to sugar.

Fried: Plantains are most often served this way. Peel and slice fruit into thin wafers. Fry in deep fat to produce "chips" or peel and slice fruit lengthwise. Fry in a greased skillet. This makes a tasty, sweet, and nutritious addition to a menu.

Baked: Peel and arrange in a greased baking pan. Brush well with melted butter. Sprinkle lightly with salt. Bake at 450 degrees for 10 to 12 minutes or until bananas are tender.

Broil: Peel and arrange on a broiler rack or pan. Coat with butter and salt lightly. Broil 3 or 4 inches from heat, about 5 minutes on each side or until browned and tender.

Frozen Puree: Mash or puree bananas, working quickly to avoid darkening fruit. Two or 3 bananas yield 1 cup of puree. Add a tablespoon of prepared syrup for each banana used. Mix, package, and freeze. Frozen puree may be used in many recipes calling for mashed bananas.

Calamondin

Calamondin is a citrus fruit, grown in South Florida and generally in season from November through March. It is a small, 1½-inch diameter, thin-skinned orange-colored fruit that resembles a miniature orange. The inner white pith is not bitter as in other citrus fruits. However, it is very acid in flavor, which prevents most people from eating it out of hand. Calamondins are also used decoratively as well as for its fruit.

The juice is highly prized for drinks.

The entire fruit may be used in making marmalade, after discarding the seeds. Other uses include desserts, sauces, and preserves.

Halves of calamondin are a treat served with seafood. Thin slices attractively garnish punch, tea, or salad dressings. The juice can be frozen in cubes and used as desired.

Carambola

1 average carambola equals 20 calories.

The carambola, often called star fruit, is a very interesting fruit, long a favorite of Southern China. South Florida's tropical climate is well suited to the production of carambola trees with a number of varieties, the best known being the Golden Star.

Carambolas average 4 to 5 inches in length and 2 inches in diameter. The fruit is most unusual as it is star-shaped when sliced. A crisp, waxy, golden-yellow skin encloses juicy pulp that in some varieties is very sour while in others is almost sweet.

Carambolas may be pickled, frozen, or preserved. However, they develop a bitter taste if cooked. The delicate, distinctive flavor is far best when used fresh.

Carambolas may be refrigerated for a week or more, but the sooner this fruit is eaten, the better.

Thin slices of sweet carambola are sparkling stars which enchant menus. Slice fruit crosswise and use in the following ways: Dip in sugar, chill, and serve as snacks; add to fresh fruit salads; float slices in a punch bowl; or garnish baked meats.

To freeze carambola, cover fresh slices with cold syrup made of equal parts of water and sugar. Pack in an airtight container, leaving ½ inch headspace. Use these frozen slices as garnishes.

Coconut

1 cup packed grated fresh coconut equals 440 calories

The coconut palm is a symbol of tropical South Florida and has been a source of nourishment for centuries.

A good fresh coconut is heavy for its size. Shake it to make sure it contains milk. Avoid cracked coconuts and those with wet, moldy eyes.

How to open a fresh coconut:

Shake the coconut. A good, mature coconut contains a large amount of liquid.

After removing the outer husk, puncture the "eyes" of the nut with a nail or ice pick, draining the milk to drink fresh or to save and use later in recipes.

To remove the shell, bake the drained coconut at 350 degrees for 20 to 30 minutes, or put it in the freezer for an hour. Then place the coconut on a firm surface, and tap the shell lightly with a hammer in several places until it cracks. Separate the pieces of meat from the shells.

Wipe coconut meat with a damp, clean cloth and trim off the brown layer with a sharp knife.

Coconut milk may be used fresh or frozen in puddings or desserts.

Coconut meat may be grated, using a medium blade in the food chopper. One medium-size coconut equals about 3 cups of packed grated coconut or 5 cups, not packed.

Clean whole pieces of coconut may be sprinkled lightly with sugar (1 tablespoon to about 1 quart of pieces) and packed into airtight containers for freezing.

To grated coconut add 2 tablespoons of sugar. Mix well and pack firmly into airtight containers, pressing out air before sealing. Coconut may be kept in the freezer for 8 to 12 months.

Grapefruit

1 white grapefruit equals 88 calories.
1 pink grapefruit equals 92 calories.
1 cup juice equals 96 calories.

The sunshine state of Florida produces almost 45% of the world's grapefruit. Available year-round, Florida grapefruit has become a versatile fruit no longer used just for breakfast.

There are two types of grapefruit: white-fleshed and pink-fleshed. The white grapefruit has honey-colored meat and bright yellow skin. The pink grapefruit has pink meat and a pink blush to the skin.

When choosing a grapefruit, the heavier for the size, the juicier it will be. Varying shades of yellow or green coloring in the grapefruit peel are determined by temperature. Cool weather gives the fruit a colorful blush, and warm weather may cause the fruit to remain green even though it is fully mature.

1 grapefruit produces 10 to 12 sections.

1 medium grapefruit produces ⅔ cup of juice.

Guava

1 guava equals 70 calories

Guava trees grow in South Florida as a cultivated tree and also widely in a semi-wild condition, with fruit maturing practically year-round. The fruit can be round, oval, or pear-shaped. Its weight when ripe can be from 1 ounce to as much as 1 pound. Skin color is usually yellow with flesh ranging from white, yellow, pink to red. The fruit can be thin-shelled with many seeds to thick-shelled with few seeds. Flavor ranges from sweet to highly acid. The aroma of ripe guavas can be strong and penetrating to mild and pleasant. Guavas are outstanding in high vitamin C content, making them an excellent substitute for orange or tomato juice.

Guavas cut in half, peeled if desired, and with the seedy central pulp scooped out are called guava shells and have many uses. The fruit may be mashed, strained, and used to make delicious ice cream, juice, jelly, chutney, and punches.

Jaboticaba

The jaboticaba tree is native to southern Brazil and produces one of its most popular fruits. In South Florida this fruit is still rather uncommon but can be grown with success. It has been tried on the markets and has been well received.

One of the most spectacular of all tropical fruiting trees, jaboticabas grow directly upon the trunk and larger branches, singly or in clusters, from the ground up. Each fruit is grapelike in appearance, with ½-inch round shapes. When ripe, jaboticabas are dark maroon to almost black in color. The pulp is whitish translucent, contains 1 to 4 seeds, is quite juicy and flavorful.

Jaboticabas are produced most of the year. They can be eaten fresh or made into jellies, syrups, jams, or wine. Both the juice and the fruit freeze well.

Kumquat

5 to 6 kumquats equal 65 calories

Three are 3 species of the kumquat grown in Florida. Nagami is the most common and also the most successful in the southern end of the state. It is oblong, approximately 1½ inches long. The orange fleshy peel is sweet and aromatic, while the pulp is quite acid.

The Marumi variety is a round kumquat, slightly over 1 inch in diameter, and deep orange in color when ripe. The juice is quite acid, while the peel is sweet and spicy.

Maiwa kumquats also are round fruits, about 1½ inches in diameter, and the peel is of an orange-yellow color when ripe. The juice is essentially acidless, and the peel is sweet.

The kumquat is a good fruit for candying, as it crystallizes well. Also frequently used as an ornamental, the kumquat is excellent for garnishes, marmalade, preserves, appetizers, for using in salads, or eating out of hand. Fresh kumquats will keep in the refrigerator for about 1 month.

Preserved kumquats are delicious in various forms as meat accompaniments.

Sliced fresh kumquats are good in Waldorf salads or fruit salads.

Lemon

1 medium lemon equals 20 calories
1 cup juice equals 61 calories

Lemons are versatile in use, reasonable in price, and deliciously refreshing. They can add color, cheer, and good eating to every day of the year.

Lemons range in size of several inches to the Ponderosa variety which is similar in size to a grapefruit. Favorite varieties include Meyer, an orange-lemon cross; Bearss, a heavy fruit with very tough skin, high in oil content; Ponderosa, actually a citran-lemon cross fruit that is quite large but can be used as a lemon substitute.

When choosing lemons, avoid those with bruised wrinkled skins. Lemons keep at room temperature 7 to 10 days. In the refrigerator, place them in a plastic bag and store in the vegetable crisper, and they will keep for at least a month.

Six medium lemons produce one cup of juice.

One medium lemon produces 3 teaspoons of grated rind.

The following are some ideas for lemons:

—Roll a lemon and insert a toothpick in one end. Remove the pick, give food a few squirts, and replace toothpick. Store lemon in the refrigerator until the next fresh squeeze is needed.

—Add fresh grated peel to puddings, cakes, sugar, icings, salad dressings to give them a personal touch and added flavor.

—Substitute lemon juice for vinegar in many recipes. It's fresher tasting.

—Make your own buttermilk by adding 1 tablespoon of lemon juice to 1 cup milk. Let stand 5 minutes before using.

—Squeeze fresh lemon juice into the poaching liquid of fish to season and to keep fish white in color.

—Place thick strips of lemon peel in a warm oven for a few minutes to dispel unwanted odors.

—Cut lemons in half and scoop out pulp. Fill with lemon sherbert and serve as a palate refresher.

Lime

1 medium lime equals 10 calories
1 cup juice equals 64 calories

Most limes grown in Florida are either the small Key or Mexican or the larger Persian or Tahiti lime.

The Key lime is a small, round lime, very popular in south Florida for use in drinks and the famous key lime pies. The greenish-yellow fruit is about 1½ inches in diameter and contains a moderate to large amount of seeds.

The green Persian lime is the one most often found on the market.

A wedge of fresh lime can go any place a lemon does, but with perhaps a bit more flare.

Lime juice may be substituted for lemon in any recipe, but use only ⅔ to ¾ as much, due to its higher acidity.

Fresh lime juice is used in place of vinegar in dressings, marinades, and sauces.

Lime wedges offer extra zest to iced tea, cold drinks, and tomato juice.

Squeezed on salads, lime juice adds taste but very few calories.

Since there is very little sodium in fresh lime juice, it can make salt free diets interesting again.

Lime juice squeezed over fresh fruit adds a nice taste and also keeps the fruit from turning dark.

Loquat

10 loquats equal 59 calories

The loquat, also called Japanese plum, is a small delicious, oval-shaped fruit 1½ to 2 inches long. It contains two or three large brown seeds. Color varies from pale yellow to light orange when ripening. The tough, slightly wooly, thick skin is easily peeled from the juicy, firm flesh of the fruit. The flavor is mildly acid, resembles that of an apple or a peach, and can be used much like an apple in baking or preserving. Florida loquats usually ripen from February through April.

Loquats are good to eat out of hand, in pies, cakes, jellies, and jams. They can also be frozen. They keep refrigerated for a short time but bruise easily.

As an average, 14 to 16 seeded and peeled loquats equal 1 cup.

Lychees

10 lychees equal 58 calories

Be prepared for a taste thrill when you first eat one of these most esteemed of all fruits. The origin of the lychee goes back 3,500 years. Today, this exotic fruit grows in Florida, rich in flavor, color, and natural beauty.

Lychees look like clusters of rough red cherries or strawberries hanging from twigs of handsome dark green trees. These approximately 1 inch round-to-oval fruits must ripen on the tree for best flavor. The red skin is thin and brittle-leathery, forming a shell, but easily pulls away with fingers to expose a delicate white flesh surrounding a single shiny dark brown seed.

The slightly acid flavor of a lychee is difficult to describe. Think of the sweetest, juiciest, most fragrant grape you can imagine, then try to make it even sweeter. Some varieties contain more sugar than others and are an excellent source of vitamin C. Lychees may be successfully refrigerated in plastic containers for 2 or 3 weeks.

Approximately 20 to 35 lychees, depending on size, equal 1 cup of peeled and seeded fruit.

Lychees are most frequently served fresh, eaten out of the shell, or shelled and added to fruit salads.

To enjoy a fresh lychee, hold it with the stem end up and gently break the skin with your fingernail. Peel the shell down and take a bite of juicy flesh.

Peeled, pitted lychees may be frozen in a sugar syrup. Slight toughening occurs, but the flavor remains excellent. Freezing a lychee in its shell seems to produce a fruit as tender as the fresh product.

A good flavor combination is lychee with papaya and pineapple.

Mango

1 mango equals 152 calories

The mango is often called the apple of the South and might well be of more importance to people of the tropics than the apple and peach are to more temperate areas.

There are many varieties of mangoes. Generally it is a medium size fruit, from 2 to 5 inches in width and 2 to 10 inches long. The skin is smooth and thick. As it ripens it turns to yellow-green or yellow-orange, often with splashes of crimson or russet red. The flesh may be a light lemon color to dark apricot.

The better varieties of mango have a rich aromatic flavor and are delicious. The most prized varieties are not very fibrous and have flesh that separates easily from the hairy seed. The least fibrous varieties of mangoes are Carrie and Kent.

If you have never handled or eaten a mango before, approach with caution, as some people are allergic to them.

Mangoes may be picked at the mature green stage. After they have ripened, they should not be refrigerated in temperatures under 50 degrees.

The mango is good at the green stage or when ripe. Green mangoes can be substituted for apples or peaches in any recipes. When green, the mango is best for cooking. It can be used for a good mock green apple pie, pickles or mock applesauce.

Ripe mangoes are good in salads, pies, sauces, breads, chutneys, and cakes. The ripe fruit can also be pickled, preserved, canned, frozen, pureed, dried, or eaten out of hand.

Try mangoes sliced and served with cream and sugar or served with cottage cheese or ice cream.

Bite-size frozen slices are good to eat frozen.

Orange

1 orange equals 73 calories
1 cup juice equals 112 calories

Any way you slice them, oranges are delicious. Each variety has a delightful aroma, beautiful color, and distinctive flavor all its own. Technically, the orange is a berry. Florida Indians during Spanish settlement were particularly fond of the bright-colored sour oranges, piercing their skins and filling them with honey. Favorite Varieties:

Navel oranges are one of the most popular because they are large and seedless. The navel has a thick skin, is easy to peel and separate, and is widely used for orange sections.

Hamlin oranges are very popular for juice.

Pineapple oranges are medium size and moderately seedy. They are prized for juice and for fresh eating.

Valencia oranges mature later than all others. They are nearly seedless, medium large in size, have a tough rind with a pebbled surface, and produce the best juice for freezing.

Temple oranges are of medium size with few seeds. They are a cross between a tangerine and an orange.

Honeybell (or Minneola) oranges are actually tangelos. This delicious fruit with a season from January to March is a cross between a Duncan grapefruit and a Dancy tangerine. The rind is deep orange in color, the flesh very juicy and tender with few seeds.

Papaya

1 medium size papaya equals 119 calories

There are many strains and varieties of this melon-like tropical fruit, and the variation in size, form, and color is remarkable. Some papayas resemble small watermelons, while others are quite small and almost round. The skin is smooth and thin. Colors range from deep orange to green. The flesh of papaya is white before maturity, turning to a rich yellow-orange as the fruit ripens. The center cavity contains pea-sized grayish-black seeds. Papaya is produced on the trees year-round in tropical Florida. Depending on the temperature, fruit may ripen without coloring, so softening is the key to ripeness. At warmer temperatures, 65 degrees or over, a yellow blush is associated with ripening.

One medium papaya yields about 1 cup of cubes high in vitamin A.

Papaya may be eaten "on the half shell" with lemon or lime juice generously sprinkled over it.

Papaya combines well with citrus fruits in salads.

The pulp combined with cream makes a delicious frozen dessert.

Sliced and seasoned like peaches, papaya may be used in pies.

Tropical Fruits
Pineapple

1 pound of pineapple equals 236 calories
1 cup juice equals 138 calories

There were pineapple farms in Palm Beach areas during the 1930s, but it was generally discovered that the climate was not suited to large scale commercial production of pineapples. Three varieties of pineapple that are grown in Florida and known for their distinct characteristics are: Red Spanish, Smooth Cayenne, and Natal Queen. Size varies from 1 to 10 pounds or more, oval to cylindrical in shape, and yellowish to orange in color.

Pineapple should ripen on the plant for maximum flavor and sugar content. It does not increase in sweetness after it has been harvested.

Judging the degree of ripeness of a pineapple requires experience and knowledge of a particular variety.

Pineapple is usually sweeter in the summer months.

A yellow rind is not necessarily an indication of a sweet or ripe pineapple.

A first-quality, well-developed pineapple is one in which the crown is small and compact.

The sound test is the most dependable guide for choosing a good pineapple. Snap the fruit with thumb and forefinger. If you get a hollow sound, the fruit is sour. If you get a dull, solid sound, the fruit is sweeter, full of juice.

Seagrape

20 to 25 seagrapes equal 26 calories

The seagrape is one of South Florida's most desirable ornamental trees. In the late summer the berries grow in long grapelike clusters but are in no way related to the grape. The fruit hangs from branches in abundance and ripens from September through October. The single stone in the fruit is large. The velvet skin has a slightly salty flavor and a light or dark purple color. The pulp is thin.

To pick seagrapes, hold a pail under a cluster and gently run a hand over them, dislodging only the ripe fruit.

Seagrapes contain just enough pectin to produce a jelly of unusual flavor. The fruit is also used for juice, syrup, and wine.

Strawberry

1 cup strawberries equals 55 calories

Although not exclusively a tropical plant, strawberries have been popular in Florida for many years and are grown on about 2,600 acres annually. This glossy red fruit is unique because it is the only one with seeds on its outside. Several varieties are grown in Florida with ranges in shape, size, and degrees of tartness. The season of production is late December through April. Botanically speaking, the strawberry is neither a berry nor a fruit. It is the enlarged stem end of the small white blossom of the plant and a member of the rose family.

Avoid berries with large uncolored or large seedy areas, as they will be poor in flavor and texture. A dull, shrunken appearance or softness indicates over-ripeness or decay.

Do not wash or stem strawberries before storing in a refrigerator. Use within one or two days. Strawberries are very delicate and highly perishable.

One quart whole fresh strawberries equals about 3 cups.

For unsweetened frozen strawberries, wash berries, remove caps, and drain in colander. Pack berries into container. For better color, cover with water containing 1 teaspoon crystalline ascorbic acid to each quart of water. Leave ½ inch space at the top. Seal, label, and freeze.

Tangerine

1 tangerine equals 39 calories
1 cup juice equals 106 calories

Tangerines are a subgroup of the mandarin orange, and most are smaller than other common citrus. They are generally easier to peel and section than oranges. The Robinson variety is one of Florida's largest tangerines. The flesh and peel are a deep orange color. This fruit matures as early as October.

Dancy tangerines mature during December and have a very loose peel and an excellent quality. The Dancy variety has a highly colored orange peel and dark orange flesh with a small amount of seeds. They are preferred to be eaten fresh.

Tangerine juice may be substituted in recipes calling for orange juice.

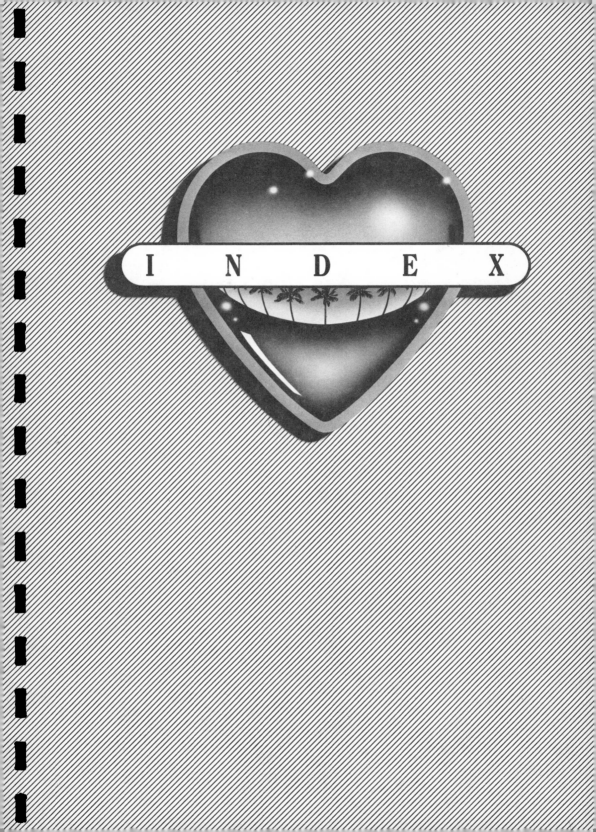

INDEX

250
Index

254
Index

258
Index

260
Index

Acknowledgements

A special thank you to A MOVEABLE FEAST, INC., Jupiter, Florida, for their contribution of recipes, and to PALM BEACH COUNTY EXTENSION HOME ECONOMICS PROGRAMS for their information and recipes on tropical fruits.

We extend much appreciation to our members and friends who shared their ideas and recipes, and to the numerous testers who were invaluable in the preparation of this book.

Elaine Albenberg
Susan Alexander
Betsy Anthony
Mary Anthony
Diane Armstrong
Bernadette Asher
Aggie Atterbury
Judy Barner
Karen Beaver
Faith Beebe
Dawn Bennett
Ginger Bills
Mary Louise Blosser
Paula Bradfield
Alice Brennan
Lynne Butler
Margo Caldwell
Patsy Casey
Susan Chambers
Connie Chauncey
Sally Cline
Carol Coleman
Julia Considine
Marty Coogler
Barbara Cooper
Cathy Costello
Lindsay Crawford
Paula Criser
Lucy Crowley
Jane Dahlmeier
Mikki D'Angelo
Judi Davis
Sue Day
Lori Donohue
Meezie Donohue
Dan Dortch
Joyce Dortch
Helen Downing
Mary Dyess
Sally Ecclestone
Gail Eissy
Ann Ellington
Jackie Fader
Glenda Feagin
Eloise Fitzsimmons
Jill Fitzsimmons
Sharon Flow
Lilly Fuller

Det Gary
Tana Gaskill
Sally Gibson
Caroline Grandy
Diann Hall
Danielle Harris
Leslie Hays
Mag Henninger
Jane Higginbotham
Patti Hill
Judy Hodge
Gale Howden
Phyllis Hughes
Betsy Hutcheon
Brooke Huttig
Ruth Jacob
Valerie Johnson
Ginny Jones
Phillis Jones
Carolyn Keathley
Joanne Keating
E.J. Lambert
Carol Leach
Nadine Livingston
Beverly Lowen
Barbara MacDowell
Margaret MacPherson
Mary Mahoney
Nancy Matson
Betsy Matthews
Ann Maus
Martha McArthur
Peggy McCarroll
Pat McIntyre
Virginia McVey
Jo Mett
Debi Middleton
Sue Milian
Carol Milling
E.J. Murray
Nancy Murray
Dale Nevenschwander
Barbara Nicklaus
Nancy Paty
Ardi Perry
Dolly Peters
Marjorie W. Pettibone
Jane Philbrick

Linda Phillips
Debbie Price
Ron Price
Sally Privett
Leslie Randolph
Sheri Reback
Archie Reeve
Mardee Reilly
Joan Renshaw
MaryEllen Rice
Monica Rich
Ann Richwagen
Betty Riggs
Lolly Russell
Kim Ryan
Bunny Schulle
Barbara Shultz
Anna DeBlock Smith
Jane Smith
Jo Smith
Sandy Smith
Barbara Sory
Ruth Spradley
Frances Stambaugh
Mary Ann Stephens
S. Michel Stewart
Janet Stingel
Sam Storm
Tottie Storm
Ann Talley
Alice Tarone
Mary Thompson
Katie Titzel
Martha Toner
Janie Vickers
Margaret Waddell
Bebe Warren
Marilyn Weber
Polly Weiss
Carol Whaley
Judy White
Korda White
Paula Willis
Montyne Winokur
Ione Wiren
Peggy Word
Trudy Word
Kathy Zullo

Heart of the Palms

Junior League Publications
P.O. Box 168
Palm Beach, Florida 33480

Please send me _____ copies of Heart of the Palms at $ 11.95 each.
Postage and handling $ 1.50 each.
Florida residents add 5% sales tax $ .60 each.
Total enclosed $_____

Name _____

Address _____

City _____ State _____ Zip _____

Make checks payable to Junior League Publications.

Proceeds will benefit the community through the Jr. League of the Palm Beaches.

Heart of the Palms

Junior League Publications
P.O. Box 168
Palm Beach, Florida 33480

Please send me _____ copies of Heart of the Palms at $ 11.95 each.
Postage and handling $ 1.50 each.
Florida residents add 5% sales tax $ .60 each.
Total enclosed $_____

Name _____

Address _____

City _____ State _____ Zip _____

Make checks payable to Junior League Publications.

Proceeds will benefit the community through the Jr. League of the Palm Beaches.

Heart of the Palms

Junior League Publications
P.O. Box 168
Palm Beach, Florida 33480

Please send me _____ copies of Heart of the Palms at $ 11.95 each.
Postage and handling $ 1.50 each.
Florida residents add 5% sales tax $ .60 each.
Total enclosed $_____

Name _____

Address _____

City _____ State _____ Zip _____

Make checks payable to Junior League Publications.

Proceeds will benefit the community through the Jr. League of the Palm Beaches.
